A twice-born faith, a rebuilt faith, is superior to an
inherited faith that has never stood the strain
of a great testing storm. If you have not clung to a
broken piece of your old ship in the dark night of the soul,
your faith may not have
the sustaining power to carry you through
to the end of the journey.
RUFUS JONES, QUAKER PASTOR

Making
Your Faith
Your Own

A Guidebook
for Believers
with Questions

TERESA TURNER
VINING

InterVarsity Press
Downers Grove, Illinois

InterVarsity Press
P.O. Box 1400, Downers Grove, IL 60515-1426
World Wide Web: www.ivpress.com
E-mail: mail@ivpress.com

InterVarsity Press® is the book-publishing division of InterVarsity Christian Fellowship/USA®, a student movement active on campus at hundreds of universities, colleges and schools of nursing in the United States of America, and a member movement of the International Fellowship of Evangelical Students. For information about local and regional activities, write Public Relations Dept., InterVarsity Christian Fellowship/USA, 6400 Schroeder Rd., P.O. Box 7895, Madison, WI 53707-7895.

All Scripture quotations, unless otherwise indicated, are taken from the Holy Bible, New International Version®. NIV®. *Copyright ©1973, 1978, 1984 by International Bible Society. Used by permission of Zondervan Publishing House. All rights reserved.*

Cover photograph: Ann Cutting/Photonica

ISBN 0-8308-2326-3

Printed in the United States of America ∞

Library of Congress Cataloging-in-Publication Data

Vining, Teresa.
    Making your faith your own: a guidebook for believers with questions/Teresa Turner Vining.
       p. cm.
    Includes bibliographical references.
    ISBN 0-8308-2326-3 (pbk.: alk. paper)
    1. Christian life—Miscellanea. I. Title.
    BV4501.2 .V476 2001
    230—dc21

                                                                                         2001024037

19	18	17	16	15	14	13	12	11	10	9	8	7	6	5	4	3	2	1
16	15	14	13	12	11	10	09	08	07	06	05	04	03	02	01			

To my son
Zephan Erik Vining,
for all the joy you've already brought me
in your twenty-one months of life.
May you grow to love God with all your heart, soul and mind.

Contents

Acknowledgments

Three years ago I went through a time of reassessment and began to reconsider why I was writing and what I wanted to accomplish. In the process of re-examination I came to ask the question, *If I could write anything right now, what would it be?* This book was my answer. Writing a book is not as solitary a process as one might believe. Many more than I could list here came alongside to help in big and small ways, but I would like at least to mention a few.

I am especially appreciative of the small crew I've come to affectionately refer to as my "staff." They tirelessly served only because of their love for me and their belief in this book. Chief among these was my mother, Linda Turner, who put helping me with this book at the top of her priority list despite other important things vying for that position. She often served as my proofreader, adviser, sounding board, babysitter and cheerleader. I am also grateful to her for passing on to me her love of the written word.

I want to thank Carol Bradburn for helping in the writing and researching process, as well as for doing many practical things that gave me time to write—including mopping my kitchen floor.

My husband, Erik, was a vital member of this book's staff, giving input, love, encouragement and patience, and serving as my personal computer systems engineer.

My sister, Jeanna Hernandez, and Jeannifer Hoskins, Audrey Kreutzer and Robin Swift cheerfully and lovingly provided childcare for my son during my writing time. I'm also grateful to Krista Stigall for her encouragement and willingness to help in whatever way necessary.

Many thanks to the members of the Heart of America Christian Writers Network (formerly the Kansas City Christian Writers Network) for their camaraderie and rich exchange of ideas.

I'd like to acknowledge all those who have helped me in my faith journey, many of whom are authors past or present whom I have never met but to whom I will always owe a debt of gratitude. They have deepened my understanding and given me hope.

Finally, thanks to InterVarsity Press and especially my editor, Cindy Bunch, who encouraged me to write this book when it was still just an idea entertained while daydreaming.

1

Somewhere Between Belief & Disbelief

*There is no weariness like that
which rises from doubting.*

ROBERT SOUTH, *eighteenth-century clergyman*

The university chapel was dark and empty, with only the evening shadows casting through the stained-glass windows and a low light glowing above the lectern. I sat alone on one of the eight wooden pews. A war was raging inside me, not just in my mind but in my whole being. I couldn't stand going on without knowing for sure, and I determined to answer the question once and for all that night.

I was supposed to be at a Bible study, and that is where I *had* been earlier, attempting to be a good Christian as I had been raised to be. The daughter of a pastor, I had always, at least on some level, attempted to do what was right. But I just wasn't sure anymore.

In the previous few months questions had been flooding my mind and sweeping away every certainty I had thought I had held securely. The atheistic worldviews held by some of my professors were having an effect on me, but that wasn't all. For quite some time there had been a gnawing uncertainty deep inside me, insistently whispering, *What if it is all a lie?*

At the Bible study all my questions had come crashing through my mind, and I hadn't been able to go on pretending I still believed. I slipped out at my first opportunity and in desperation made my way to the chapel.

There I determined to settle the question. If God were real, I reasoned, *surely* he could find a way to reveal himself to me. I wasn't asking to see an angel or to hear him speak audibly. Anything at all would do—a sense of peace, a flicker of the light above the lectern, the arrival of another person who would give me some encouragement. Anything!

I decided I was not going home until I had come to a resolution. But only silence answered my prayers, and I felt more alone than I ever had before. A cold fear began creeping into my heart as the minutes ticked by. *What if he really wasn't there?*

Grasping for a last shred of hope, I opened my Bible randomly and prayed that God would cause it to fall to something that would speak to me. But the pages opened to an obscure passage from which I could not garner one iota of meaning. It was over, I resolved. I had laid everything on the line in search of God and found nothing.

Tears ran down my face as I returned to my empty apartment. Lying in bed surrounded by darkness, I tried to grasp the significance of it all. There is no God, I told myself. This life is all there is. No one really knows why we are here or how we got here. There is nothing more than self-centered, imperfect humanity in which to hope. There is no real meaning, no basis for knowing what is right and what is wrong. It doesn't matter what we do or how we live. There is no foundation, no right and wrong, no hope.

No! something deep inside of me screamed. It could not be true. I couldn't believe that life was just a sick joke with humans and their capacity for love, appreciation of beauty, and need for meaning as the pitiful punch line. That went against all my experience as a human being. There had to be *something* more!

That night was the beginning of a new no-holds-barred search for truth in my life. If Christianity wasn't true, I wanted to know so I could go on to seek truth somewhere else—because the one thing I *did* know after that night was that I couldn't believe this life is all there is. Something deep inside me seemed to testify that somehow "good" is better than "bad" and "love" is better than "hate," and that meant we must be something more than just a sum of atoms.

That experience initiated a commitment to begin searching for answers as if my life depended on it. And this search became the pathway for me to return to Christianity with hard-won answers, able to call Christianity my own faith, not just the faith of my family, friends or church.

What About You?

Do you have questions about the truth of Christianity?

☐ Are you a committed Christian who sometimes wrestles with doubts?

☐ Are you often overcome with uncertainty when you attempt to explain to others why you believe?

☐ Or are you even among those who were raised in the church but now seriously doubt the truth of any of it?

If so, you are not alone. Every Christian I have ever been close enough to ask has admitted to me that they have struggled with doubt, at least to some degree. In fact Gary Habermas, author of *Dealing with Doubt*, claims doubt may be the single most widespread problem among Christians today.[1]

If not confronted, doubt can be debilitating in the life of a Christian. It robs us of our peace and joy and hinders our relationship with God—after all, how can we devote ourselves to knowing someone we are not sure exists? And even in small doses it can undermine our greatest intentions to tell others about our faith. If you are a Christian struggling with doubt, you probably know this all too well. If Christianity is true, however, the devastation of doubt if you are an unbeliever is even greater—it can keep you from having a relationship with the only true God of the universe.

But when allowed to drive us to earnest inquiry, doubt can be an avenue to deeper faith. A vibrant faith can never successfully be grounded in hearsay, habit or the faith of others. A faith strong enough to overcome doubt and help light the world must be a faith of our own, forged in the furnace of

> Each of us should examine the foundations of our own faith. Why do we believe God is there? Why do we believe God is good? How do we know Jesus ever lived? How do we know Jesus rose from the dead? Why do we trust the authority of the Bible? How do we understand that Christianity is true? . . . Answers to such questions are no substitute for faith. But without the answers to such questions faith may be no match for doubt.
>
> OS GUINNESS[2]

honest seeking and tested in the laboratory of real life. Daily we are confronted with a dizzying variety of alternative belief systems and sometimes even hostility toward traditional faith. Now more than ever we need to know not only *what* we believe but also *why* we believe it.

Some Faces of Doubt

My husband's friend Cody was raised in a strict Christian home. He rebelled in high school but always believed he would come back to the God of his childhood. However, the longer he stayed away and hung out with people who didn't believe, the more questions he had about the validity of Christianity. Now he is married with a young family, trying to figure out how to raise his children. It seems as if he should have them in church. But he wonders about all the errors people say are in the Bible. And is it even possible to know if a religion is really true?

Nina is the wife of a pastor. In a rush of enthusiasm she became a Christian in early adulthood; she even attended a Christian college. But after years of hard service in the church, she sometimes wonders if God is really there. Why does he sometimes let such horrible things happen in the world? And why is the Bible so confusing at times?

Jeff, one of our neighbors, has always attended church and lived a fairly moral life, but he has held back from making a real commitment to Christianity. As an intellectual, he knows there is always much more to learn about any subject—how can he really know enough about Christianity to make a decision? Isn't it good to keep your options open? And doesn't the Bible contradict science?

Using This Book

This book is designed to help you forge a vibrant faith. Of course the very fact that you are experiencing doubt means that you are uncertain about the truth of Christianity. My purpose here is not to convince you of the truth of Christianity at all costs. Obviously my search for truth has led me to believe in Christianity. But if I were wrong, I wouldn't want to lead you to follow in my error. My desire, instead, is to help you evenhandedly examine the evidences for Christianity so you can make your own decision.

This book provides an overview of the major areas of support for Christianity and basic responses to some of the chief arguments against Christianity. It is meant to help you work through the process of determining exactly what you believe and why. Questions are sprinkled throughout the text to help you think through the points raised and decide about them for yourself.

> The real community of man . . . is the community of those who seek the truth, of the potential knowers.
> **ALLAN BLOOM**
> (University of Chicago professor of social thought)[3]

Along the way you'll find quotations of people from a variety of walks of life and different eras. Endnotes are provided in case you want to do further reading. Where it seems relevant, I have provided some background information about the individuals quoted.

I urge you to scrutinize the information presented in each chapter for any facts or reasoning you question. Information generally means little to us unless we evaluate it, seek further clarification if necessary, and then either reject it or accept it. This book will be useful to you only in proportion to your willingness to explore your questions and seek out the facts or insights you need to settle them.

I promise you that I will never knowingly present faulty evidence to try to make an argument stronger. However, if you come across a statement you question, I encourage you to do further study and come to your own resolution. And feel free to contact me at my website <www.yourownfaith.com>. I would love to hear from you.

Your Companion Journal

This book is designed for you to use with a journal. Depending on your preference, you can use anything from a spiral notebook with your name scrawled on the front to an embossed journal from a card shop. Your journal will serve you in several ways.

Define your questions clearly. Identifying specific questions is the first step to answering them. Sometimes when I am struggling with doubt, I feel overwhelmed by so many questions I can't even begin to deal with all of them. However, when I actually sit down to identify what they are, most of them boil down to only a handful of major issues. Once I identify what my questions really are, I don't feel so overwhelmed, and I can begin searching for answers.

Keep a record of your process of investigating your questions and an account of the answers you found. I heard of an old farmer who continually doubted that he was really a Christian. He couldn't believe that God had forgiven him for his past sins. For him, it came down to needing something tangible. He decided to drive a stake in the ground inscribed with the date he had asked Christ for forgiveness. After that, when he began to wonder if he was really a Christian, he went out and looked at the stake to remind himself that as of that date his sins *were* forgiven.

Like the farmer's memorial stake, your journal can serve as a weapon against future doubts by documenting the decisions you make about what you believe and the basis for them. When doubt threatens your beliefs again, you can turn to your journal to remind yourself of the foundation on which your beliefs are based.

Scattered throughout this book you will find a graphic of a stake beside a question that calls for a decision. When you have established what you believe about that point, you can write out your answer in your journal and mark it in some way. These marks will signify that you believe you have truly addressed the question and are confident in the decision you have made.

Record questions for future study. Finally, your journal can serve as a springboard for future study. I pray that in working through this book you will obtain a solid foundation for belief in Christ, but I am not foolish enough to think all your questions will be answered. All *my* questions are not answered, and I don't expect some of them will ever be answered in this lifetime.

> Ask and it will be given to you; seek and you will find; knock and the door will be opened to you. For everyone who asks receives; he who seeks finds; and to him who knocks, the door will be opened.
> MATTHEW 7:7-8

We can't expect God to answer all our questions. "The secret things," Deuteronomy 29:29 says, "belong to the LORD our God." However, I firmly believe God will give you enough answers to establish your faith securely if you really want them. "Every time in the Bible when a person is called upon to exercise faith," writes Josh McDowell, "it's an intelligent faith. Jesus said in John 8, 'You will know the truth,' not ignore it."[4]

When you come upon questions that lie beyond the basics necessary for faith, record them in your journal so you can go back and investigate the issues in more detail later. We may never receive complete answers to some of our questions, but the more we seek God through studying the areas in which we still have questions, the more we can hope to know him better and help others know him better. As C. S. Lewis says, "Where we find difficulty, we may always expect that a discovery awaits us."[5] Recording your questions and delving into them more thoroughly later will help you begin unearthing discoveries God has for you.

To get the most from this book, before beginning the next chapter get a notebook or journal to record notes, questions and insights.

As you read, you may want to take notes on the most important points of each chapter so you can go back and remind yourself of them later. You also may want to write the answers to questions in complete thoughts so you can go back and read your journal without having this book open.

Using this Book in a Group Study

This book is designed to be used equally well in an individual or a group Bible study. The questions in each chapter, in addition to helping you work through the information, make great discussion questions for groups.

Here are a few reasons you may want to consider going through this book with one or more other people:

☐ The accountability provided by a group can be an important factor in keeping you motivated.

☐ Encouragement from others can give you hope when you are struggling with tough questions and discouragement.

☐ In a group you have the benefit of hearing the comments of others who may tackle a question differently than you do or have different insights.

> The kingdom of heaven is like treasure hidden in a field. When a man found it, he hid it again, and then in his joy went and sold all he had and bought that field.
>
> MATTHEW 13:44

Worth the Cost

As you work through this study, you may sometimes feel discouraged. Sorting through what you believe can be hard. You may start wondering if answers are really out there and if it is worth the effort anyway.

But what if it is true that the God of the universe loves you and wants to have a relationship with you? What if it is possible to work through your doubts and become confident in what you believe? What if God can become so real to you that others can't help but see him in your life? Wouldn't you hate to give up and keep stumbling along with your questions when answers were within your reach? Wouldn't that possibility alone be worth the effort?

The Bible tells us, "Love the Lord your God with all your heart and with all your soul and with all your strength and with all your mind" (Lk 10:27). Unfortunately, I wouldn't say this describes most Christians, but it can describe you and me if we want it to. Being willing to invest the time to become convinced of what we believe is a crucial step in that direction.

 Begin your journal by answering the following questions:

What part is doubt playing in your life right now?

What are some questions you have struggled with about Christianity?

What is your response to the biblical command to seek truth with all your heart, soul, mind and strength?

Grappling with Doubt

You will seek me and find me when you seek
me with all your heart.

JEREMIAH 29:13

W hen I began struggling with doubt, I felt I faced an unscalable wall. I knew the Bible says that without faith it is impossible to have a relationship with God, but nobody ever seemed to be able to tell me how to *get* faith if I didn't have it.

Every time there was a sermon on faith, I would listen intently, hoping the speaker would actually tell me what to do if I found myself lacking in faith. Unfortunately all the sermons I heard concentrated on the importance of faith, which, in my opinion, any child in Sunday school could have told me. They never explained how I could muster faith if I already knew I needed it. Apparently faith was something either you had or you didn't, and I obviously didn't because I was constantly hounded by doubts and questions.

That kind of reasoning led me to a riddle I couldn't solve. It seemed that either faith was something God granted arbitrarily at some magic moment to some people and not others or faith was something some people just had naturally from birth, just as some people naturally have dimples or blue eyes. In either case, it didn't matter how much I wanted faith; if I didn't have it, there was nothing I could do. And this left me back staring at the wrong side of a rock-hard wall.

Have you ever wrestled with what to do when you find yourself lacking faith? If so, what were the circumstances? Have you ever heard someone teach on this? If so, what did they say?

Cracks in the Wall

Around this time I stumbled onto Jeremiah 29:13, which says, "You will

> Come to me, all you who are weary and burdened, and I will give you rest. Take my yoke upon you and learn from me, for I am gentle and humble in heart, and you will find rest for your souls. For my yoke is easy and my burden is light.
> MATTHEW 11:28-30

seek me and find me when you seek me with all your heart." At this point my doubts were so strong I couldn't have said for sure whether I even believed the Bible to be true. However, this verse gave me a glimmer of hope that if it *was* true I wouldn't be stuck on the wrong side of the wall forever, as long as I was willing to search for God with all my heart.

I found the same promise in Matthew 7:8: "For everyone who asks receives; he who seeks finds; and to him who knocks, the door will be opened." And as I looked closer, I began to see it threaded throughout the entire Bible.

I also found the Bible mentioned some surprising instances of people who seemed to suffer from doubt—people Jesus didn't just send away empty-handed. When John the Baptist was in prison, he sent a delegation to Jesus to ask him if he was the Messiah or if they should look for another (Mt 11:2-3). That sounded like doubt to me. And of course Thomas, one of Jesus' own disciples, didn't believe the others when they told him about the resurrection (Jn 20:25). Another man who brought his son to Jesus to be healed said, "*If you can do anything*, take pity on us and help us" (Mk 9:22, emphasis added). That sounded like the kind of pitiful statement I might have made. Later this same man cried out to Jesus, "I do believe; help me overcome my unbelief!" (Mk 9:24), echoing the contradiction I found in my own heart.

In none of these cases did Jesus turn the doubter away. Jesus told John the Baptist's friends to go tell John about all the miracles people were experiencing as evidence that he was the Messiah. To Thomas, Jesus stretched out his hands and let him feel the nail prints. And to the man with the sick son, Jesus showed his power by healing his child.

 Do you believe the Bible teaches that if we sincerely seek God we will find him? Why or why not?

Which of these New Testament doubters do you identify with most?

Based on Jesus' response to these doubters, how do you think he would respond to your doubts?

The Nature of Faith

These examples of New Testament doubters helped me begin to see three things about faith.

1. *Strong and weak faith.* Faith isn't some magical substance that we either completely have or completely don't have. And the existence of doubt doesn't necessarily mean the absence of all faith. If the man with the sick son had had *no* faith, he would not have brought his son to Jesus. And if *I* had had *no* faith, my doubts wouldn't have bothered me and I wouldn't have been scouring the Bible and listening to sermons trying to find the remedy.

2. *Seekers welcome.* God doesn't arbitrarily turn people away for flunking the faith test. We may have faith at differing levels at different times, and as long as we are committed to seeking God, we can trust him to give us what we need to strengthen our faith. Faith is a gift from God, but the Bible indicates it is a gift freely given to those who seek it. That doesn't necessarily mean we can expect God to appear physically to us or show us an obvious miracle when we doubt, but it does mean that somehow, though perhaps in a different way than we expect and in different timing, he will give us what we need for faith.

3. *Not just a blind leap.* I had heard faith defined as belief in something

you have no reason to believe, and I couldn't understand why God would value such a leap against the intellect. To hold that kind of faith seemed comparable to my randomly choosing some stranger off the street to put in charge of everything I own—or worse yet, my family's safety. Who in their right mind would do that? And if faith was like that, how was I supposed to decide which religion to blindly follow? Under the blind leap system I could just as easily follow Buddha or Muhammad as Christ. How could I know which was true?

But the accounts of doubters in the Gospels helped me see that the faith taught in the Bible is actually rooted in fact. Each time doubters came to Jesus, he gave them something to help their unbelief. To John he gave the evidence of his miracles. To Thomas he gave the evidence of the nail scars. And to the father of the sick son he gave the evidence of a healed son.

 Describe a time when your faith was strong and another time when it was weak.

In what ways have you been encouraged when your faith has been weak?

Have you heard faith defined as believing something you have no reason to believe? If so, where did you hear that, and what was your response?

Do you agree with the three observations about faith stated here? Why or why not?

The Reason in Faith

You may be surprised to hear that the Bible teaches that faith is grounded in facts. Many people characterize faith as being both illogical and anti-intellectual. However, the Bible depicts its message as something that can be supported by evidence and understood by the mind.

> Jesus replied, "Go back and report to John what you hear and see: The blind receive sight, the lame walk, those who have leprosy are cured, the deaf hear, the dead are raised, and the good news is preached to the poor."
> MATTHEW 11:4-5

☐ In Isaiah, God invites the Jewish people to come and *reason* with him (Is 1:18).

☐ Jesus instructs his disciples to love God with all their heart, soul and *mind* (Mt 22:37; Mk 12:30; Lk 10:27).

☐ After explaining salvation through Christ to King Agrippa, Paul pleads with him to seriously consider his words and adds, "What I'm saying is true and reasonable" (Acts 26:25).

Faith is an act of the whole man, not of his understanding alone, but it is precisely because it is an act of the whole man that it includes the understanding.
OS GUINNESS[1]

☐ In his letter to the Philippians, Paul describes his job as "defending and confirming the gospel" (Phil 1:7).

☐ Peter instructs Christians to "always be prepared to give an answer to everyone who asks you to give the reason for the hope that you have" (1 Pet 3:15).

 Do you agree that biblical faith is based on evidence? Why or why not?

The Trust in Faith

But saying that the faith taught in the Bible is based on fact does not imply that faith ends there. It is as if fact is the root system for faith—the basis—and the spiritual working out of that faith is the tree.

Having faith isn't really like putting a stranger in charge of everything I own; it is more like what I did when I married Erik. He gave me good reason to believe that I could trust him as my husband, but it was still a matter of faith for me to make those vows. On our wedding day I could not *prove* to myself or anyone else that Erik would fulfill his part of the commitment. I just had to trust him to do so based on the integrity and love he had demonstrated in the three years we'd dated.

As Clark Pinnock says in *A Case for Faith,* "Faith . . . does not involve a rash decision made without reflection. . . . It is the act of wholehearted trust in the goodness and promises of the God who confronts us with his reality and gives us ample reason to believe that he is there."[2]

Christianity is based on evidence. It is reasonable faith. Christian faith goes beyond reason, but not against it.
PAUL LITTLE[3]

 Describe some instances in your life when you have demonstrated a fact-based faith in someone or something.

So Why Do Christians Struggle So Much with Doubt?

I used to have a disturbing suspicion that the very existence of doubt in my life and in the lives of other Christians was surely a strong argument against Christianity. Why would committed Christians continue to question the very basis of their faith? Why would God allow doubts to cripple Christians even after they have decided to follow him? The only reason I could think of was that perhaps God is truly not there and we are just attempting to convince ourselves of some extravagant fairy tale.

Needless to say, many skeptics would agree heartily with this reasoning. But since that night in the chapel I have stumbled onto another possible explanation. I couldn't see it at the time, but looking back I am amazed to discover that it was actually my doubts and questions that drove me to become more serious about my faith and led me to a deeper, more meaningful relationship with God.

I suspect that if God had simply revealed himself to me during my experiment in the chapel, I would not have begun seeking him wholeheartedly, as I did in his silence. Things that come easily are too easily taken for granted. I never spent more time praying or prayed more sincerely than when I faced the true implications of believing God did not exist.

> Just as the Christian has his moments when the clamour of this visible and audible world is so persistent and the whisper of the spiritual world so faint that faith and reason can hardly stick to their guns, so, as I well remember, the atheist too has his moments of shuddering misgiving.
> C. S. LEWIS (twentieth-century Christian writer and former atheist)[5]

"A twice-born faith, a rebuilt faith," a Quaker pastor named Rufus Jones wrote, "is superior to an inherited faith that has never stood the strain of a great testing storm. If you have not clung to a broken piece of your old ship in the dark night of the soul, your faith may not have the sustaining power to carry you through to the end of the journey."[4]

Doubt actually can work to drive us *toward* God if we let it. It can motivate us to reexamine our foundation to make sure it is not faulty, and it can be a doorway to new insights that we never would have unlocked otherwise.

This is especially important for those who have grown up in the church as I did. Since my earliest awareness I had accepted Christianity based on the faith of my family. If I was going to take my faith seriously, it was inevitable that a time would come when I would have to examine Christianity for myself to see if I actually believed its claims. This is a more difficult process for some than for others, but all of us must go through it if we are to develop a mature faith. And this testing of our faith will continue throughout our Christian experience to nudge us out of our comfort zone and challenge us toward continued growth. As Gary Parker writes in *The Gift of Doubt:*

> Doubt occurs when the certainties that we have always trusted tremble and shift beneath us. Doubt represents a searching out of these certainties to make sure they're solid enough to support us. It means we allow ourselves to question the previously unshakable truisms of our faith to test their firmness under our feet. And this testing is not necessarily harmful. Indeed, it might only warn us to move toward safer, more secure ground.[6]

 How do you usually respond when you encounter Christians with doubts?

Do you agree that doubt can have a positive effect? Why or why not?

Describe some things you have had to put effort into that have become more valuable to you because of this effort.

What insights, if any, have you gained through struggling with doubt?

A Sad Football Story

But the power for good that doubt can have in our lives comes only in the strength and insight we gain in confronting it. If we are wrong about what we believe, doubt can be the agent that drives us to discover our fallacy. If we are correct, doubt can be a catalyst compelling us to confirm our beliefs and gain an even greater understanding of them. But if doubt is left unaddressed, any benefit goes unrealized, and it can become a destructive force.

> If a man begins with certainties he shall end in doubts; but if he be content to begin with doubts, he shall end in certainties.
> FRANCIS BACON (seventeenth-century English philosopher and statesman)[7]

When I was a junior in high school, our football team somehow managed to win enough games to go to the state championship. But the state challengers were a much better team than we were. The players and students alike went to the game full of school spirit and naive confidence, but within the first few minutes of the game, the other team scored two touchdowns. Things went downhill from there. By the end of the game our team had given up and was just meandering around the field waiting for the clock to run out while the other team scored touchdown after touchdown.

An athletic team can do any of three things when confronted with imposing challengers.

☐ They can recognize the threat and train harder than ever to enable them to win against the challengers. (That is what our team *should* have done before the state championship.)

☐ They can go into denial and ignore the threat, attempting to convince themselves and others that there is no real challenge. (This is what our team *did* do before the championship game.)

☐ Or they can become so intimidated by the threat that they give up before the fight has even begun. (This is what our team did *at* the game that made it such an embarrassment.)

We can choose to face the challenge our doubts bring, we can live in denial pretending as if our doubts do not exist, or we can give up before we give faith a chance. Only in the first of these options can true resolution and peace be found.

 Describe a time when you reacted to some difficulty in each of the three ways listed above. What was the outcome in each case? Which of these options are you most naturally inclined to when dealing with doubt?

The Strategy

The first step in overcoming doubt is to earnestly commit ourselves to seeking truth. As mentioned earlier, the Bible makes it clear that God wants you to seek him with all your heart, soul, strength and mind, and that when you do, he will reveal himself to you. This is a spiritual attitude of making the search for truth a priority in our lives and committing ourselves to accept truth when we find it.

> Doubt is an incentive to search for truth, and patient inquiry leads the way to it.
> G. BAILY
> (nineteenth-century journalist and abolitionist)[8]

This attitude makes sense regardless of whether you believe Christianity is true right now. If we really want to know if Christianity is true, it is only reasonable to try doing the things the Bible indicates will help us in finding God. And even if Christianity is not true, it only makes sense that if there is any god out there and if there is anything we can do to discover that being, it would begin with committing ourselves to the quest.

The second step is to roll up our sleeves and begin firmly establishing what we believe about spiritual things and why. And that is what the rest of this book will help you do.

 Do you agree that these two steps are a good strategy for confronting doubt? Why or why not?

 Do you believe the Bible teaches that if you seek God you will find him? Why or why not?
Do you believe the faith taught in the Bible is a faith based on fact? Why or why not?

Digging Deeper

The Gift of Doubt: From Crisis to Authentic Faith *by Gary E. Parker (San Francisco: Harper & Row, 1990). This is an encouraging book, delving into the reasons for doubt and the definition of faith, written by a pastor who has struggled with doubt himself.*

Love Your God with All Your Mind: The Role of Reason in the Life of the Soul *by J. P. Moreland (Colorado Springs: NavPress, 1997). Moreland examines the role the mind plays in all areas of the Christian life and offers instruction on how to use our minds more effectively.*

Thoughts on Thinking

But How Can We Really Know Anything?

A mind that questions everything, unless strong enough to bear the weight of its ignorance, risks questioning itself and being engulfed in doubt.

ÉMILE DURKHEIM, *founder of modern sociology*

How can we really know anything? I hadn't really thought about this question until I began trying to figure out what I believed. Then I was surprised to find it standing squarely between myself and the answers I longed to find.

After that night in the chapel I decided to start from scratch and determine what I believed without taking anything for granted. But when I started trying to think through my doubts, each question just led to another question until I felt as if I were on some giant, out-of-control merry-go-round. And in the center of all the confusion seemed to be this surprising issue of how I could hope to know anything.

How can I know there is a God? I would ask myself. Then I would consider some basic fact that seemed to support belief in God—like the existence of right and wrong.

But how do I know there really is such a thing as right and wrong?

Because something deep inside me tells me this is true.

But how do I know I can trust this sense inside of me?

This is where things started spinning. *Uh—I'm not sure.*

And how can I even know that the things around me are as they seem?

Well . . . ?

With so many people believing so many different things, how can I be arrogant enough to think my own thoughts can lead me to real truth?

> As never before, we [in the postmodern world] are sensitive to how hard it is (some would say impossible) to know truth. We are increasingly aware of the ways our presuppositions and subjectivity color our perception, understanding, and communication of "the truth"—and as a result, we aren't at all sure if what we have at the end of the day is even worth calling "truth."
> BRIAN D. MCLAREN[1]

After a few such internal conversations I realized it was impossible to begin establishing what I believed about God until I thought through what I believed about the possibility of *knowing*. I began to see that all beliefs must have some point of reference, involving basic principles about the possibility of knowing. Most of us don't contemplate these much. We just take them for granted. But recently a subtle shift has occurred in popular thinking—and without our even realizing it, this shift can undermine our confidence in our ability to know things.

 Have you struggled with questions about how we can know things? If so, in what ways?

What would be your response to someone asking the kinds of questions raised here?

The Basis for Knowing

When you think about it, it seems almost too basic to mention that the way we know things is through the experiences we have (whether that is encountering information in a book or feeling the sensation of falling in love) and the inferences we make from them. How do I know it is cold outside? I can see frost on the window, I can feel the sting of cold air on my face, and I can read the thermometer, which says it is below freezing.

This process of drawing inferences and conclusions from experiences and known facts is what we call "logic" or "reasoning," and it is so ingrained in us that we automatically use it without even realizing it. Logic involves an intricate set of interrelated principles about reality that help us make sense of the world around us—like the principle that if there are only two options and we find the first isn't true or does not apply, then it must be the second.

Our reliance on reason is based on three assumptions: that reality makes sense, that we can generally trust the experiences we have, and that we can generally trust the inferences our minds make from these experiences. But many today are questioning these assumptions, and I found this questioning was at the center of my confusion.

Define logic in your own words.
Do you agree that logic is based on the three assumptions listed here? Why or why not?

Why Trust Reason?

One English professor I had openly spurned logic. I can still see her in my mind, her gray hair pulled tight in a bun and her bright skirt swaying back and forth as she pounded the table, railing against the narrowness of "Western thought." Her class always left me feeling slightly confused. If logic was invalid, why did she grade our essays on "cohesiveness"? And didn't she use logic in her own arguments against the use of logic?

Although I had wrestled before with whether to trust the assumptions of logic, I couldn't accept her way of thinking. In fact, after considering it I decided to embrace the use of logic in my search for truth for a number of reasons.

☐ I could see our minds *automatically* use reason to make deductions and decisions.

☐ I could see that it is impossible to function without the use of reason, and that reason seems to be the only tool we have available to make judgments. In fact, I found I couldn't even get away from the use of reason when deciding whether to trust my reasoning.

☐ I also saw that reason seems to lead to real answers. The things my reasoning told me made living on a daily basis possible. When I saw frost on the window, it usually did mean I needed to wear a coat. And when I reasoned through other things, whether in school, work or relationships, it usually led me to real insights I could use.

☐ I also could see that reasoning is what makes all areas of study possible and that all advancements for humanity involve the use of reason—like advancements in medicine, communication and food production.

☐ But the final deciding point was that I saw that rejecting reason would be choosing to slam the door on any possibility of making sense out of life or anything in it. If I was wrong to trust my reasoning and everything was totally different from the way I perceived it to be, then I had no hope of making sense of the world anyway. Since I had no proof that my reasoning could *not* be trusted, and since the only alternative I saw was to accept hopelessness, I decided I had nothing to lose and everything to gain.

 Do you agree that it is impossible to function without the use of reason? Why or why not?

What is your response to the statement that to choose not to trust our reasoning is to choose hopelessness?

But I'm Not Greek!?

One misunderstanding about logic is that the Greeks invented it and that it is just one thought system. The Greeks did study logic and codify it, but logic, in the general sense, existed long before they began giving it attention. Reason has existed throughout history and has been present in every invention and forward stride humanity has ever made.

If Everyone Uses Reason, Why Don't We All Agree?

Although we all use reason every day to function, we don't necessarily always use it well.

☐ Sometimes we don't discipline our minds to think through things.

☐ Sometimes we let what we want to be true dictate what we believe to be true.

☐ Sometimes we make judgments based on incorrect assumptions.

☐ Sometimes we use circular or other unreliable arguments.

The process of human knowing is complex, and often our individual perceptions, partialities and desires can cloud our thinking. But I don't believe this means we should throw out logic altogether; instead we should learn to use it more effectively, for it is in learning to use it more effectively that we can overcome many of these problems. "The main value of logic," David Kelley notes in *The Art of Reasoning*, "is that it helps us stay in touch with the facts."[2]

Logical Equals Unemotional?

Many times we assume that a logical person is someone who is uninvolved and unemotional. But being rational doesn't have to mean this. Someone with strong emotions doesn't necessarily have to be illogical, and a logical person doesn't have to be unemotional.

"On the contrary," David Kelley writes, "there is no reason we cannot have both: clear, logical minds, and passionate feelings."[3]

Do you agree that reason helps us stay connected with the facts? Why or why not?

Why is it important to stay connected with the facts?

Why do we often assume an emotional person can't be logical? Describe a person who is both passionate and logical.

But Doesn't Faith Contradict Reason?

Many who do not believe in the supernatural believe that reason and faith are hopelessly at odds, but I have found this view can usually be traced back to three misconceptions.

1. *A misunderstanding of the nature of faith.* As noted in the last chapter, if faith is "believing what we know is not true," then reason and faith *are* in contradiction. But if faith is "the act of wholehearted trust in the goodness of God who confronts us with his reality,"[4] then there is no contradiction. Faith transcends reason, but it does not oppose it.

2. *A lack of understanding of the necessity of faith in all areas of knowl-*

edge. Many people do not realize that some faith is involved in everything we know—at the minimum faith in our own reason. As Brian McLaren explains:

> None of us lives with absolute, unassailable certainty about anything; we all live by faith. What we might call practical certainty . . . is really relative certainty, shot through with faith on many levels. Even the skeptic can only doubt one set of propositions because he believes another. Without some structure of faith . . . we can't get anywhere. We're like weightless, tractionless runners or boxers. We have no leverage. So, some degree of faith is downright inescapable, and faith runs through all we claim to know.[5]

3. *An assumption that the natural world is all of reality.* Another reason many of us believe faith and reason are contradictory is that we begin with the basic assumption that the world we see and touch is all of reality. If we accept this assumption, religious faith *is* a contradiction to reason. But do we have adequate grounds to assume this?

> We cannot arrive at faith on the back of reason alone. . . . But reason can act as the vehicle that drives us into a place from which we can see the possibility of God. And if we believe that God created our minds for his purposes, it makes sense that God would encourage us to use our rational powers to better understand his personality.
> GARY PARKER[6]

What evidence do we have that the natural world we see and touch is all there is? What about people throughout history who have insisted they have encountered something outside this natural realm? Is it more reasonable to believe that supernatural events never happen even though many have claimed to experience them, or is it more reasonable to consider the possibility that there is a reality beyond this world? These are questions we all must answer for ourselves, questions we will investigate further in later chapters.

How would you characterize the relationship between faith and reason?

Name two things you consider to be obvious and explain how you know them to be true. If you look at these explanations closely, can you see where faith factors in? If so, how?

Do you believe it is valid to assume that the natural world we see and touch is all of reality? Why or why not?

Digging Deeper

Come Let Us Reason Together *by Norman L. Geisler and Ronald M. Brooks (Grand Rapids, Mich.: Baker, 1990). An easy-to-understand Christian introduction to logic.*

The God Who Is There *by Francis Schaeffer (Downers Grove, Ill.: InterVarsity Press, 1968). This book offers a philosophical discussion of the recent shift in popular thinking regarding the subject of knowing.*

But Is There Really Truth to Be Found?

Of course the discussion of how we can know things brings up another question, one that has turned all arguments upside-down in recent years. The reason many of us are questioning the possibility of knowing is that many of us are asking *whether real truth actually exists for us to know*. Belief in relativism has permeated modern societies so much that it is difficult sometimes even to recognize it in ourselves. Relativism teaches that there is no absolute truth—that what is true for you is not necessarily what is true for me.

A Philosopher's Ideal?

The term absolute truth sometimes conjures up visions of some philosophical ideal succinctly chiseled on great tablets of stone far away on a wind-swept mountain ledge. But belief in absolute truth is not nearly this dramatic. It simply indicates belief in an independent, objective reality—that is, a reality that exists outside of ourselves and doesn't change dependent on what we think about it.

At first glance relativism seems appealing. It relieves us of the difficulty of having to find truth because it sets each of us up as the author of what our truth is. We can invent a worldview that appeals to us, and we don't have to worry about others disagreeing with us or having to correct others if we don't agree with them because each invents his or her own reality. I often struggle with this when I get lost browsing the shelves of a mega-bookstore. So many sincerely believed ideas are represented that it is tempting to want to be able to accept them all as true. But relativism isn't quite as uncompli-cated as it may seem.

Describe some circumstances when you have encountered belief in relativism.
What has been your response to relativism?

The Inconsistency in Relativism

If we are going to hold to relativism, we have to be willing to say that all beliefs are equally true and no action is absolutely wrong. This may be fairly simple when stated in general terms, but it becomes impossibly complex when we begin thinking about specific examples.

What about the beliefs of a racist, cult leader or tyrannical dictator? Are we really willing to say these people's beliefs are equally valid to our own?

According to relativism should we have any societal standards of behavior? Is there anything we can legitimately expect people to do or not to do?

What if someone murders a person we love? Are we willing to say that although we abhor murder it may be OK for others because their truth may be different?

Even if we try to rescue some societal standards by claiming that there are some behaviors we just can't allow because they aren't good for society, would this argument be consistent with relativism? According to relativism wouldn't we have to admit that perhaps what I feel is good for society is not what someone else would feel was good for society—for example, that what would be a good society for an ax murderer might be to have no laws and live according to the survival of the fittest?

This demonstrates one of the foremost problems with relativism: the fact that none of us, no matter how adamantly we insist on belief in relativism, can actually live consistently by it. This inconsistency can be seen in the way those who believe in relativism act on a daily basis. When they are injured, they insist on justice, even though under relativism "justice" cannot be defined in such a way that it applies to anyone other than yourself. When they are discussing whether God exists, they say, "He may exist for you, but he doesn't for me." But when wondering whether their spouse is cheating on them, they say, "Tell me the truth. Either there is someone else or there is not!"

When you think about it, this inconsistency is present even in the very definition of relativism in that the statement of the philosophy actually contradicts itself. People who insist that it is wrong to believe in absolutes and that all truth is relative are actually presenting an absolute. They are insisting that their view of the world is right and the view of someone who believes in absolute truth is wrong.

What is your response to the statement that it is impossible to consistently adhere to relativism?

Relativism and Reason

I find I function every day on the premise that reality exists regardless of what I believe about it. I might sincerely believe that I can walk through walls, but if I try to demonstrate this, I'll get a bruised forehead. If Erik and I disagree about what time a concert starts, we can't just say we both are right. We have to call to find out what reality is. It would be ridiculous for us to say that the concert starts at a different time for each of us depending on our private beliefs.

One of the fundamental principles of logic we use every day is that if one thing is true, then the opposite cannot also be true. If I am married, I can't also *not* be married in exactly the same way. If my favorite ice-cream flavor is chocolate mocha, then it cannot also be true that my favorite ice cream flavor is *not* chocolate mocha. If I exist, then it cannot also be true that I do *not* exist.

> At the end, nobody can see anything except himself.
> ... There are so many realities that in trying to encompass them all one ends in darkness.
> PABLO PICASSO
> (pioneer of modern art)[7]

That is the way reality functions, and I see no evidence that it would be any different for the big questions of life—questions like whether there is a God. If I believe that an all-powerful God created us and loves us and sent his Son two thousand years ago in real history to die for us and you don't believe this, reason tells us only one of us can be right.

Do you agree that relativism contradicts reason? Why or why not?

A Fairy Tale with a Not-So-Happy Ending

Relativism seems to be a pathway that in the end leads away from hope to meaninglessness. For isn't saying that each of us can have our own truth really the same as saying reality only exists in each of our minds? And if reality only exists in our minds, isn't that the same as saying it doesn't really exist at all? If reality doesn't exist at all, what meaning can we possibly have in our lives? If we each live in our own invented reality, what point of connection can we hope to make with each other? If my "good" happens to be your "bad," how can we even hope to communicate with each other? How can we have any standards for behavior or hope to have any shared sense of meaning?

 Do you agree that belief in relativism leads to despair? Why or why not?

Some have stated that belief in relativism contributes to increased suicide and violence. What do you think about this statement?

Can you think of areas in your life where your thinking has been affected by relativism? Explain.

Where We All Must Begin

In any search for truth we must begin with either a conscious or unconscious confidence in the belief that truth does exist and that it is possible to use our minds to help uncover it. Without belief in truth we are left adrift, helplessly launched on a journey without a destination. Without belief in reason we are left with the possibility of a destination but without a compass to direct us there, desperately chasing our own wake with no idea of which direction to turn. It is only after we establish that a destination of truth does exist and that our reason can serve as a compass to help get us there that we are able to truly begin our search.

> The despair of modern man ... is despair in depth in that it tends to use formulations and forms which seem to give hope and yet in the nature of the case lead to more profound depths of despair.
> FRANCIS SCHAEFFER[8]

Tell of a time when you were lost with no sense of direction. How would this experience correspond to what it is like when someone disregards reason as a means to truth?

What is your response to the statement that believing in relativism is like being on a journey without a destination?

Do you believe that you should trust reason in your search for truth? Why or why not?

Do you believe in absolute truth? Why or why not?

Digging Deeper

Choosing My Religion *by R. C. Sproul (Grand Rapids, Mich.: Baker, 1995). This little book examines the question of absolute truth in a fast-paced conversational format.*

True for You, but Not for Me *by Paul Copan (Minneapolis: Bethany House, 1998). Copan addresses relativism and related beliefs and summarizes the arguments against them.*

The Brushstrokes of God

Is There a Creator?

The heavens declare the glory of God;
  the skies proclaim the work of his hands.
Day after day they pour forth speech;
  night after night they display knowledge.
There is no speech or language
  where their voice is not heard.

PSALM 19:1-3

When I was growing up, my family lived outside a small town in southeast Kansas, and I used to take long walks through the fields surrounding our home. I remember standing in a pasture watching as imposing waves of thunderclouds began rolling in, tumbling over each other as the bluegrass swayed back and forth in the wet wind and birds chirped their wild warnings.

I remember catching a sunset just as it exploded in the sky in a fiery display of crimson and fuchsia, as fireflies darted back and forth in the disappearing light and the sound of locusts echoed through the trees.

I remember walking in the evening after a snowstorm when the sky was an endless purple and ice crystals outlined each branch of every tree. The darkness of the sky was reflected in the snow with a shimmering bluish-purple cast, and the whole world was silent except for the shuffle of my footsteps.

At times like these my heart involuntarily rose within me, and I couldn't escape the impression that although no one was around, I was not alone—the impression that somewhere sharing this moment with me was the ultimate Artist who made all of this, using only his own imagination and creative power.

 Have you ever received this impression when observing nature? If so, describe some of these times.

The First Question

It seems that no question is more fundamental in any search for truth than whether we and our world are the creation of a supreme being. And no question has more far-reaching implications. After that night in the chapel, I discovered that if I didn't believe in anything beyond this world, that decision would affect my entire view of life and set me on a totally different path.

Though simply believing in a "higher being" is still far removed from believing in the God of the Bible or any other faith, it is an indispensable prerequisite. And yet this basic question is often at the crux of our doubts. It is almost as if an echo from doubters around the world can be heard asking, "But how can we even know there is a God?"

> More consequences for thought and action follow from the affirmation or denial of God, than from answering any other basic question.
> MORTIMER ADLER (twentieth-century American scholar)[1]

The more firmly we establish the answer to this question, the more stable our faith will become. But how can we even begin to answer such a momentous question? In my own life I discovered it was the silent witness of the universe that became my foundation in answering this question.

Think of two people you know—one who sincerely believes in God and one who doesn't. What difference does it make in their lives?

Have you ever struggled with the question of how we can know God exists? If so, in what circumstances?

Evidence of Design?

By the time I began struggling with doubt, my meandering walks and youthful impressions of nature had all but slid from memory. I was busy with school, friends, work and the tough business of trying to figure out life. But as I began focusing on the search for truth, I was drawn to long walks once more—this time in city parks and playgrounds. Concrete and telephone poles weren't enough, however, to hide the grandeur, and I was once again overcome with the artistry of the universe. A deep conviction in the existence of the Artist became the first stone in rebuilding my faith.

Hardly anyone would disagree that we find ourselves surrounded by a natural world of awesome beauty, complexity and magnitude. The intricate design of a snowflake, the powerful interrelationships of the oceans, grasslands and mountains, the delicate biological systems involved even in the simplest organism—all these, even after centuries of study, still escape human comprehension and present the inevitable question of how this all came to be.

> My religion consists of a humble admiration of the illuminant superior Spirit who reveals himself in the slight details we are able to perceive with our frail and feeble minds. That deeply emotional conviction of the presence of a superior reasoning power, which is revealed in the incomprehensible universe, forms my idea of God.
> ALBERT EINSTEIN[3]

Many have dismissed the complexities of the world as merely an effect of random mechanical processes, but for others that explanation is simply not adequate. Sir Isaac Newton wrote, "This most beautiful system of the sun, planets and comets, could only proceed from the counsel and dominion of an intelligent and powerful Being."[2] Even Charles Darwin concedes in his *On the Origin of Species,* "To suppose that the eye, with so many parts all working together . . . could have been formed by natural selection, seems, I freely confess, absurd in the highest degree."[4]

Many scientists believed that the introduction of the theory of evolution would bring about the end of all controversy about a "higher being." But the opposite has happened. As Patrick Glynn, a scholar and former atheist, explains in *God: The Evidence*, "Modern thinkers assumed that science would reveal the universe to be ever more random and mechanical; instead it has discovered unexpected new layers of intricate order that bespeak an almost unimaginably vast master design."[5]

Physicist Paul Davies is among those who have been affected by these findings. He writes:

> I belong to the group of scientists who do not subscribe to a conventional religion but nevertheless deny that the universe is a purposeless accident. Through my scientific work I have come to believe more and more strongly that the physical universe is put together with an ingenuity so astonishing that I cannot accept it merely as a brute fact. There must, it seems to me, be a deeper level of explanation.[6]

 Do you agree that an intricate design gives evidence of a designer? Why or why not?

Made for Life?

The artistry was what first struck me, but I also began to see other things in the world that seemed to point to a supreme being. One of these was the fact that not only does the world seem to manifest an intricate and complex design but it also seems to be strangely put together for the specific purpose of producing life. Scientists call this observation the "anthropic principle," and since its formal introduction by astrophysicist Brandon Carter in 1973, the implications of this principle have rocked the scientific community and refueled the debate about the existence of God in mainstream science.

"Beginning in the 1960s," Patrick Glynn explains, "scientists began to notice a strange connection among a number of otherwise unexplained coincidences in physics. It turns out that many mysterious values and relationships in physics could be explained by one overriding fact: Such values had been necessary for the creation of life."[7] Since the 1960s many more "lucky accidents" in our universe have been found, contributing to the acceptance of this baffling concept.

What were the chances that all these variables would lock into place at precisely the right time to produce exactly the right universe in which life would exist? Consider nature's four fundamental forces: gravity, electromagnetism, and the strong and weak nuclear forces. "Every one of these forces," states physicist Richard Morris, "must have just the right strength if there is to be any possibility of life."[8] And "luckily" they do. This is just one small example of the "fine-tuning" necessary for life to exist. Some scientists have compiled long lists of such "cosmic coincidences."

These observations have brought a variety of responses. Some scientists simply shrug their shoulders and say that of course all these coincidences would have had to converge or we would not be here to talk about them. But others don't find it so easy to dismiss.

In an attempt to avoid any supernatural explanation, some scientists have proposed that there perhaps are an infinite number of universes and so it can be expected that in at least one of them the right variables would come together to produce life. Many unsolved problems still exist in this proposed explanation, however, not the least being that there are no scientific data to support it. A person "might find it easier to believe in an infinite array of universes than in an infinite Deity," according to Paul Davies, "but such a belief must rest on faith rather than observation."[10]

Some have gone so far as to suggest that the universe has actually caused itself in some quasi-life-force way to develop in such a manner that life could flourish. Another group projects that perhaps our descendants will continue to develop into higher and higher life forms so that they will become like gods and create the necessary conditions for life *in their and our past.*[11] But some are accepting the anthropic principle as evidence of what some religions have claimed all along—that a Creator God designed the universe specifically to nurture life.

Physicist and theologian John Polkinghorne writes, "The theistic conclusion . . . can claim serious consideration as an intellectually satisfying un-

> Yet as biochemists discover more and more about the awesome complexity of life, it is apparent that the chances of it originating by accident are so minute that they can be completely ruled out. Life cannot have arisen by chance.
> FRED HOYLE (astronomer)[9]

derstanding of what would otherwise be unintelligible good fortune. It has certainly struck a number of authors in this way, including some who are innocent of any influence from a conventional religious agenda."[12]

A Home Prepared

When we brought our newborn son home from the hospital two years ago, we had already spent months preparing for him. Child locks, toys, a dresser full of tiny pajamas, a bassinet for sleeping, pacifiers for sucking, diapers for changing, a rocking chair for rocking—all these things greeted him at his arrival. Thinking about all the preparations in nature to support our lives reminds me of this—air for breathing, water for drinking, sun for warming, soil for growing and exquisite sunsets that seem to exist for no other reason than to lift the soul.

 What is your response to the observation that the world seems to be specifically put together in a way to nurture life?

In the Beginning?

Another characteristic of nature that I found pointing to a supreme being involved the need for a beginning and a first cause. The prevailing view among scientists used to be that the universe was eternal, that it had existed for an infinite number of eons in the past. But this view has almost unanimously changed in the last century. Now, primarily based on two discoveries, most in the scientific community agree that the universe *had* to have a beginning.

When Einstein first proposed his relativity theories in 1915, he assumed the current view of a static, eternal universe. Yet under this assumption he had to add a "cheat factor" to his theories to account for why the universe did not collapse in on itself. He couldn't explain why this factor was necessary. Then in 1927 evidence was uncovered suggesting that the reason the "cheat factor" had been necessary was that the universe was actually expanding.

If I were a religious man, I would say that everything we have learned about life in the past twenty years shows that we are unique, and therefore special in God's sight. Instead I shall say that what we have learned shows that it matters a great deal what happens to us.
JAMES TREFIL
(physicist)[13]

The consequences of this discovery were far-reaching: if the universe was expanding, it was not possible that it has existed forever. For if the universe is expanding in all directions as it seems to be, then by playing an imaginary video of the history of the universe in reverse in our minds, we can see that if we put no limits on the age of the universe, there would be a time when all matter would come together into an infinitely dense ball. And scientists agree that an infinitely dense ball has no volume; it is the same as nothing.

The Logic of an Eternal Past

In addition to scientific evidence, a few philosophers have proposed some convincing arguments that it is not logical to think the universe could have existed forever in the past. For one of these arguments see the essay "The Finitude of the Past and the Existence of God" by William Lane Craig in Theism, Atheism and Big Bang Cosmology.[14]

The second discovery that caused scientists to change their minds about the universe's being eternal has to do with the second law of thermodynamics. Briefly stated, this law asserts that heat flows spontaneously from hot entities to cold entities and never from cold to hot. Davies explains:

> This law is therefore not reversible. . . . Scientists were quick to draw the conclusion that the universe is engaged in a one-way slide toward a state of thermodynamic equilibrium. This tendency toward uniformity . . . became known as the "heat death." . . . The fact that the universe has not yet so died . . . implies that it cannot have endured for all eternity.[15]

So why does it matter that the universe had a beginning? The implications are significant. If the universe had a beginning, the next logical question would be what caused that beginning. And this question has led many back to the concept of a Creator.

C. D. Broad, a twentieth-century philosopher, writes:

> I must confess that I have a very great difficulty in supposing that there was a first phase in the world's history, i.e., a phase immediately before which there existed neither matter, nor minds, nor anything else. . . . I suspect that

my difficulty about a first event or phase in the world's history is due to the fact that, whatever I may *say* . . . I cannot really *believe in* anything beginning to exist without being *caused* . . . by something else which existed before and up to the moment when the entity in question began to exist.[16]

> There is a kind of religion in science; . . . every event can be explained in a rational way as the product of some previous event; every effect must have its cause. . . . This religious faith of the scientist is violated by the discovery that the world had a beginning under conditions in which the known laws of physics are not valid. . . . Science has proven that the Universe exploded into being at a certain moment. It asks, What cause produced this effect? Who or what put the matter and energy in the Universe? . . . And science cannot answer these questions.
> ROBERT JASTROW
> (astronomer)[17]

This question becomes even more intriguing when we consider Einstein's laws of relativity. According to the scientific evidence on which these laws are based, space and time are inseparably linked. That means the beginning of the universe was also the beginning of all space and time. But this raises a critical question: if the beginning of the universe was also the beginning of all space and time, what would have existed to cause this beginning to happen? This strangely points to the idea of a transcendent God—a God existing beyond space and time who created the universe out of nothing, the very picture the Bible has presented for thousands of years.

Some have asked why, if the issue is that everything must have a cause, we don't ask who caused God. Isn't it just as difficult to imagine a being without cause as a universe without cause? But this question reflects an improper understanding of the above data. Inherent in the very definition of a Creator God is the concept of an uncreated Creator existing outside of our time and universe—for if this being created our time and universe, how could this being exist within it? And if God exists outside of our time and universe, then God is not subject to the cause-and-effect laws of our universe.

What possible explanations can you think of for why the universe would suddenly explode into existence before any space, time or matter existed?

Do you agree that if the universe had a beginning this would point to the possibility of a Creator? Explain.

Using Science to Find God?

Some question the use of scientific findings to support belief in God. After all, if a theory were presented tomorrow that offered a scientific explanation for the beginning of the universe or the anthropic principle, would I become an atheist?

Human understanding is always imperfect and continually changing as it grows. Our belief in God shouldn't rest solely on scientific findings. But this doesn't mean we should overlook the fact that some of the latest scientific findings actually support the existence of God. This is noteworthy, especially for those who are afraid they cannot believe in God because of science. Currently no scientific finding disproves the existence of God, and there are many findings that raise the possibility.

The Artist Behind the Masterpiece

When visiting the Nelson-Atkins Museum of Art in Kansas City once, I was particularly struck by a huge wall-sized Monet painting. The gigantic swirls of blue, green and purple were overpowering, but as I looked closely, it occurred to me that despite the magnitude of the painting I could still see the individual brushstrokes of the painter—an unmistakable connection with the artist behind the masterpiece.

When it comes down to it, I find only two possible explanations for all the beauty and grandeur of our universe—a natural explanation or a supernatural explanation. Either the universe came into existence solely by blind natural phenomena or it was the creation of a supreme being. It seems significant that the majority of people throughout history have believed in a god or gods. Even in our "scientific age," only 6 percent of Americans are atheists or agnostics.[18] Romans 1:20 says that the universe proclaims God's "eternal power" and "divine nature." I myself find this to be undeniably true.

Other Options?

A life-force? *Some add another option to the two I have mentioned and insist that perhaps it wasn't a supreme being but rather some kind of "life-force" at work in the universe. But as C. S. Lewis explains in* Mere Christianity, *"when people say this we must ask them whether by Life-Force they mean something with a mind or not. If they do, then 'a mind bringing life into existence and leading it to perfection' is really a God, and their view is thus identical with the Religious. If they do not, then what is the sense in saying that something without a mind 'strives' or has 'purposes'?"[19]*

Aliens? *Some movies and television programs have popularized the theory that perhaps beings from another world were behind the development of life on earth. But this theory doesn't answer the questions raised in this chapter; it just moves them back one step. How did these creatures come into being, and who created their universe?*

On a scale from one to ten, how convincing do you find the natural evidences for a Creator? Explain.

Do you believe the natural world points to the possibility of a Creator? Why or why not?

Digging Deeper

God and the Astronomers *by Robert Jastrow (New York: W. W. Norton, 1978). Written by an agnostic scientist, this short book will give you a taste of the scientific debates surrounding the issues discussed in this chapter.*

God: The Evidence—The Reconciliation of Faith and Reason in a Postsecular World *by Patrick Glynn (Rocklin, Calif.: Prima, 1997). This is an intriguing and easy-to-read book by a former atheist about some of the most recent evidence for the existence of God in natural science, psychology and medicine. The first chapter deals exclusively with the ramifications of the anthropic principle mentioned here.*

Show Me God: What the Message from Space Is Telling Us About God *by Fred Heeren (Wheeling, Ill.: Searchlight, 1995). Heeren offers a much more detailed look at the subjects discussed in this chapter, including interviews conducted with leading scientists.*

Mirrors of Our Maker

Does Belief in God Fit with What We Know About Ourselves?

*So God created man in his own image,
in the image of God he created him . . .*

GENESIS 1:27

W hen I was about ten, I overheard someone tell how my great-great-grandfather had committed suicide by hanging himself in his barn. Of course I had never met this man, but the fact that one of my direct ancestors had thought life so bad that he preferred to be killed by his own hand often disturbed me. At that age I couldn't fathom the complexities of life that would ever bring someone to such a point.

Not until much later, as I sat in a discussion on the "human predicament" in a literature class, did I really begin to grasp the hopeless confusion that being human can cause. As humans we long for meaning but are unsure of whether real meaning is even possible. We have great potential for good but also great potential for cruelty that persists in shocking degree despite all social progress.

No society has been able to abolish human sadness, no political system can deliver us from the pain of living, from our fear of death, our thirst for the absolute.
EUGÈNE IONESCO
(Theater of the Absurd playwright)[1]

As humans we long for connection with others but are often frustrated and disappointed in our interactions with family and friends. We have a capacity for great joy but also for mind-searing grief and pain. We long for immortality but live with the knowledge that someday we will die.

As humans we often know the right thing to do but wind up doing the opposite, despite all the guilt and consequences. Our imaginations can fathom accomplishing great things, but many times we are trapped in circumstances over which we have little control and find it a challenge just to get through the day. And all for what?

 What situations in life cause you to think about the paradoxes involved in being human?

The Missing Piece?

After putting words to the dilemma in my literature class, I realized that I had often unconsciously railed against some of these same things— attending a family reunion where everyone seemed to be talking but no one seemed to be saying anything, watching forlorn people at a carnival chase the next thrill, visiting a rest home where pictures of proud, beautiful people hung in rank-smelling rooms inhabited by bent and broken shadows.

As I read more widely, I discovered that the struggle against the contradictions and complexities of humanity runs throughout both modern and ancient literature. These paradoxes have confounded writers throughout the ages and caused many to stagger to the conclusion that the human dilemma is outside comprehension and hope.

But then I encountered a few authors who seemed to point to a tiny shaft of light that although didn't illuminate all the answers, at least gave the questions a different shape. What if all the contradictions were not just meaningless paradoxes in nature but were meant to point us to something beyond? Could introducing God into the equation begin to make sense of the puzzle of humanity?

When we are searching for truth, it makes sense to examine the one thing we can reasonably hope to know best: ourselves. In my own search the evidence from nature first persuaded me of the existence of a God, but the evidence from human experience confirmed this and led me to a deeper conviction of what that God must be like. Specifically, I found five human characteristics that cry out for belief in God.

 Have you noticed characteristics in humankind that seem to point to the existence of God? If so, explain.

The Miracle of Our Minds

Human minds appear to be uniquely designed to understand the world around us. If we are simply a highly evolved collection of molecules responding to stimuli, the amazing correspondence between the development of our minds and the laws of the universe is unfathomable.

"Scientists themselves," acknowledges physicist Paul Davies, "normally take it for granted that we live in a rational, ordered cosmos subject to precise laws that can be uncovered by human reasoning. Yet why this should be so remains a tantalizing mystery. Why should human beings have the ability to discover and understand the principles on which the universe runs?"[2]

Consider our ability to do higher math or to understand the intricacies of an atom. Some would say this ability, which no other species in the animal kingdom even comes close to possessing, simply developed through natural selection in the evolution process, which brings about change in a species based on survival benefits. But in the real world can we really imagine that being able to understand these things would give enough of a survival benefit to warrant its selection?

As scientist John Barrow writes in *Theories of Everything*, "Why should our cognitive processes have turned themselves to such an extravagant quest as the understanding of the entire Universe? . . . None of the sophisticated ideas involved appear to offer any selective advantage to be exploited during the pre-conscious period of our evolution."[3]

From a naturalistic point of view I found the remarkable effectiveness of the human mind inexplicable. But when I considered the possibility that we and the universe may have been created by a rational God who chose to create human beings in his image, the fog seemed to clear. If this was the case, it made sense that our minds would run along the same lines as the laws of the universe—since the human mind would be a minuscule reflection of the mind of God.

What do you think about the naturalistic explanation for the effectiveness of our minds?

If you had to come up with a survival benefit for the human capacity to understand higher math, what would some possibilities be? Explain whether you believe any of these benefits would warrant selection in a preconscious period of evolution.

Do you think the "unreasonable effectiveness of our minds" points to the possibility of a Creator? Why or why not?

The Likelihood of Loveliness

Another mystifying characteristic of human existence that seemed to me to point to God is our appreciation of certain "lovely" things—the fragrance of a rose, the splendor of a sunset, the captivating tones of music. It almost seemed as if much in the universe was created expressly for our enjoyment.

> The "unreasonable effectiveness of mathematics" in uncovering the structure of the physical world . . . is a hint of the presence of the Creator, given to us creatures who are made in the divine image.
> JOHN POLKINGHORNE
> (physicist and theologian)[4]

While I could see that some of the things we appreciate could be said to have evolutionary benefit—for instance, that we often find those of the opposite sex pleasing to look at—this explanation was insufficient to account for the majority of lovely things. "The poverty of an objectivistic account," as John Polkinghorne writes, "is made only too clear when we consider the mystery of music. From a scientific point of view, it is nothing but vibrations in the air, impinging on the eardrums and stimulating neural currents in the brain. How does it come about that this banal sequence of temporal activity has the power to speak to our hearts of an eternal beauty?"[5]

For me, it came down to whether it is more reasonable to believe that our appreciation of beauty is just a meaningless evolutionary fluke or that this might be an eternal pointer to the existence of a Creator who also appreciates beauty and lovingly created these things for our pleasure.

Think of four things you consider "beautiful," and list any possible natural explanations for your appreciation of each of them.

Do you believe that our appreciation of beauty points to the possibility of God? Why or why not?

The Puzzle of Our Personalness

Another characteristic that cried out to me for belief was the "personalness" of humanity. As seventeenth-century philosopher and scientist Blaise Pascal marveled, despite our insignificance in physical scale, we are greater than all the stars because we alone can know about them and ourselves. We alone are self-aware.

Regardless of how much we admire the intricacies of animal interaction, it is impossible not to see the wide gap that separates us from all other creatures. We alone are capable of higher thinking and communicating. We alone possess the capability of making a wide range of conscious choices in behavior. We alone develop elaborate religious, legal and historic traditions. We alone invent and manipulate advanced technologies. We alone write volumes exploring the questions of what and why and how.

> [Naturalism] offers what professes to be a full account of our mental behaviour; but this account, on inspection, leaves no room for the acts of knowing or insight on which the whole value of our thinking, as a means to truth, depends.
> C. S. LEWIS[6]

Many scientists attempt to tell us that the observation that humanity is personal and different from the rest of the animal kingdom is only an illusion. All people and animals, they maintain, are simply combinations of molecular processes responding to stimuli in the only way they can. The problem with this theory, however, is that if humans are just a collection of molecular processes programmed to respond in certain ways with no real choice, then how can we, as programmed creatures, presume to say that what we believe to be true about reality is even meaningful?

I found this concept confusing when I first encountered it. But when I thought about it, it made sense. In these scientists' view, aren't the scientists themselves just a collection of molecules? And how can it make sense for any collection of molecules, responding to stimuli in the only way they can, to propose a meaningful explanation of the real nature of themselves? These scientists' own view undermines their right to hold it.

> The hypothesis for the origin of consciousness in Darwinian evolution would not account for the highest levels of consciousness in *Homo sapiens*. . . . The uniqueness of our experienced self has not been given an acceptable materialist explanation. . . . Since materialist solutions fail to account for our experienced uniqueness, I have proposed . . . that it is necessary to postulate a supernatural creation for each human self, which is a mystery beyond science.
> JOHN C. ECCLES (winner of 1963 Nobel Prize for physiology and medicine)[7]

Despite their own outlook, these scientists live each day as if they were personal beings, making real conscious choices—not just responding to stimuli—and as if they were capable of discovering real truth about themselves and the world around them. Ironically, we can't escape our own personalness even when we deny it.

So if we are personal beings, I found myself asking, where did this "personalness" come from? Is it realistic to think that an impersonal universe gave rise through random chance to such a complex consciousness? What would be the evolutionary benefit to such personalness—which introduces the phenomenon of suicide, completely contrary to the survival instinct? On the other hand, isn't it possible that our own personalness points to the existence of a personal, self-aware God?

 What do you think about the statement that humans are personal beings?

If humanity is personal, do you think the naturalistic or the supernatural view best accounts for this? Why?

The Mystery of Morality

After the evening in the university chapel I was an atheist for about two hours. As pitiful as this may sound, that was as long as I could hold to that belief system. One of the major reasons was an unshakable conviction in the existence of a true morality.

I could not have explained it cohesively that night. But something deep inside of me told me that "good" is better than "bad" and "love" is better than "hate," and I sensed that that had to mean that something exists beyond ourselves. I have thought about this much more extensively since that night and have come to believe it even more strongly.

This conviction was particularly reinforced recently when I read a passage by philosopher Bertrand Russell explaining his atheistic beliefs:

> That man is the product of causes which had no provision of the end they were achieving; that his origin, his growth, his hopes and fears, are but the outcome of accidental collocations of atoms; that no fire, no heroism, no intensity of thought and feeling, can preserve any individual life beyond the grave; that all the labours of the ages, all the devotion, all the inspiration, all the noonday brightness of human genius are destined to extinction in the vast death of the solar system . . . only within the scaffolding of these truths, only on the firm foundation of unyielding despair, can the soul's habitation henceforth be safely built.[8]

These words made it clear to me that the atheistic view leaves no room for a true morality. Yet in another work Russell attempts to give value to our moral sense: "It is these things that make the unique importance of man, and it is of these things that each generation in turn is the trustee. To hand on the treasure, not diminished, but increased, is our supreme duty to posterity."[9] But according to Russell's own view, what really would be the difference between right and wrong? What motivation would there be to choose right? What meaning would this even have? And what would be the sense in speaking to an "accidental collocation of atoms destined for extinction" about duty?

On the other hand, if a higher being exists, this does give a foundation for belief in a true moral duty. If we are creations of this being, it makes sense that our moral code would be based in this being's character. The supernatural view introduces the possibility of our being more than just a "collocation of atoms" and the prospect that we may possess real significance, we may live beyond the grave, and what we do really may matter.

Other Explanations for Our Moral Sense

Those who argue our moral sense does not reflect a true right and wrong, and so doesn't point to a Creator, usually explain our moral sense in one of two ways.

1. Cultural norms. *Some say our moral sense is just a set of cultural norms passed down from parent to child. But two major problems exist with this explanation.*

The moral codes of all societies throughout recorded history are amazingly similar, despite incredible cultural diversity.[10]

Those who hold this view have to be willing to say, without reservation, that no activity is intrinsically wrong and such things as bigotry, murder, rape and child abuse are just a matter of cultural preference and would be OK to practice in another society. This runs so contrary to something deep inside humanity that most of us, when it comes down to it, can't accept it.

2. Herd instincts. *Others say our moral sense is a set of "herd instincts" that have developed in the human animal over time, encouraging peaceful communal living that aids in survival. But problems exist with this explanation as well.*

We all know what it is like to have an instinct to do something. It is a strong urge we feel, like the urge to eat when we are hungry. But our moral sense is different; it often tells us to do things we do not feel like doing—such as to refrain from lying even when lying would help us.

Our moral sense often judges between which instincts we should follow. For example, if we see someone in trouble, we may experience two instincts—one to stop and help and one to run the opposite direction. It is our moral sense that judges between these two and tells us that we should help even if our urge for self-preservation is strong. And even though we may choose not to follow our moral sense, deep down we always know we should have helped.

With this explanation as well, we would have to accept without reservation that no true right and wrong exists.

 Do you think our moral sense points to the existence of God? Why or why not?

Eternity in Our Hearts

Every once in a great while I stumble into one of those moments in life—an almost-perfect moment that I long to hold on to, an almost-glorious moment saturated with a beauty so near it makes my soul ache, an almost-wondrous moment that explodes with joy because I know that this is finally nearing life as it *should* be, but also throbs with pain because I know it is life as it

never really *will* be, and that even this moment is
already gone.

> He has also set eternity in
> the hearts of men . . .
> ECCLESIASTES 3:11

The ache of wanting to capture a sunset. That
catch-in-your-throat, I-don't-ever-want-to-let-go feel-
ing when your two-year-old gives you a hug. That instant of nostalgia that you
get in the middle of a quiet evening with close friends.

For me, such almost-moments accentuate another great mystery of life.
Everyone I talk to seems to possess a yearning for something beyond what
they experience day to day. A profound thirst for connection, perfection and
immortality seems to dwell in each of us. It seems none of us can escape the
notion that we were made for something much more than we currently possess.

I can find no natural explanation for this. Why would we develop hunger
for impossibilities? Why would our hearts become set

> You awaken us to delight
> in Your praise, for You
> made us for Yourself, and
> our hearts are restless
> until they rest in You.
> ST. AUGUSTINE (fourth-
> century theologian)[11]

on an elusive ideal so foreign to us it is impossible to
even articulate? Where do religious yearnings come
from, and why does a belief in the afterlife persist in
almost every society? All other appetites have a cor-
responding reality to fulfill them, but not this one, unless—unless, as I have become convinced, there is a
reality beyond what we can see and touch. For this hunger seems to whisper
of paradise and eternity and unimaginable beauty.

 Have you experienced these kinds of impressions? If so, when?
Do you agree that these may be indications that there is
something beyond the reality we can see and touch? Why or why
not?

The Need for More

Even if the information we receive from nature and ourselves points to the
possibility of a higher being, if we stop here we are left with many
questions and much confusion. From our personalness we can deduce that
the higher being is personal. From the composition of our minds we can
deduce that this being appreciates beauty and rational thought. From the
insistence of the moral code we can deduce that this being is very in-

terested in how people behave toward one another.

But we are still left wondering who the higher

> Do you not know?
> Have you not heard?
> The LORD is the
> everlasting God,
> the Creator of the ends
> of the earth.
> ISAIAH 40:28

being is, why this being created us and our world, and what this being's relationship is to us now. Even if we are led to the belief that a higher being exists, we are hopelessly lost at this point unless this higher being somehow gives us a way to find out more. And it is not unfathomable that the higher being would do just that if it wants to be known by us.

This is exactly where Christianity and many other religions claim to come in. They teach that the higher being *does* want to be known and has given more specific revelation. Christianity claims this revelation is the Bible.

In my own search I first came to the determination that whether Christianity was true or not, I believed in some kind of a Creator. Then I couldn't help but notice that this Creator seemed to share at least some characteristics with the God described in the Bible. And this sent me back to take a closer look at the Bible to see if I could trust it as a revelation from God.

Of course this process wasn't nearly as tidy as it sounds. I jumped back and forth in my thinking and took many detours and loops. But I kept coming back to the solid assurance that yes, I did believe in God, and yes, many of the things I saw in myself and in the world pointed to a God very like the one I had learned about in Sunday school. And this kept prodding me to examine the claims of Scripture, as we will do in the next chapter.

What do you think about the statement that if a supreme being exists, it is reasonable to believe this being might find a way to communicate more about itself to us?

In what ways do the characteristics in humanity and in nature discussed in the last few chapters point to a God resembling the one of the Bible?

Do you believe the natural or supernatural view offers the best explanation for human nature? Why?

Do you believe Christianity offers viable explanations for the peculiarities we see in human experience and for this reason deserves a closer look? Why or why not?

Digging Deeper

Mere Christianity *by C. S. Lewis (New York: Macmillan, 1952). This book offers the most perceptive discussion of the evidence for God based on the morality of humanity I have found. It is the classic most people refer to when discussing this topic.*

He Is There and He Is Not Silent *by Francis A. Schaeffer (Wheaton, Ill.: Tyndale House, 1972). Another classic and one of Schaeffer's easier books to read, this book serves as a great introduction to Christian answers to the questions raised in this and the previous two chapters.*

Reliable, Relative or Ridiculous

Can We Trust the Bible?

One of the most significant of all themes to the Christian is that of the inspiration and authority of the Bible. The truths concerning God, Christ and salvation are surely of supreme importance. But how can we get to know these truths if it is not by means of the Scriptures themselves?

RENÉ PACHE, *The Inspiration and Authority of Scripture*

The words I read felt like a rockslide plummeting down on me, with each word taking an emotional toll. I was sitting in the recliner in our family room, surrounded by books arguing against the reliability of the Bible. Although I had come far in my faith since that day in the chapel, the accumulated force of the downpour threatened to bury me in self-doubt.

I felt a jumble of anger and fear. Could it really be possible that the Bible was nothing more than an unreliable copy of religious propaganda written by impostors who knowingly invented its contents out of a mixture of elaborate legends and thin air? Could it really just be a collection of books randomly chosen by a group of fallible men who imposed them on others? How could these authors say such things about the book that had shaped my entire life? And how did I know that what they said wasn't true?

What are some criticisms you have encountered about the Bible? From whom have you heard them, and what effect have they had on you?

What would be your response to someone struggling with questions about the reliability of the Bible?

Truth or Tall Tales?

If our search for truth has led us to consider the God of Christianity, then it only makes sense to take a closer look at the book on which Christian beliefs are founded. Belief in the Bible as inspired revelation from God has been at the heart of historic Christianity. But in light of modern scholarship, is it really possible to still believe in the divine inspiration of Scripture? Is the Bible historically reliable? Where did the Bible come from? How do we know that the books included are the right ones? Do our modern versions accurately reflect the original texts? And does this book really show signs of being divinely inspired?

List the claims the Bible makes about itself in these verses: Matthew 5:18; 2 Timothy 3:16; 2 Peter 1:16-21; 2 Peter 3:15-16; Revelation 1:1-3.

A Quick Overview

☐ *The Bible was written by more than forty authors, including kings, priests, fishermen and peasants, over hundreds of years, with each book functioning separately within its time frame as well as collectively with the other books as they came to be included.*

☐ *It was written using three languages: Hebrew, Greek and Aramaic.*

☐ *The Bible contains a variety of literary genres popular in their authors' day, such as historical accounts, prophecies, parables, letters, songs and proverbs. Some books also incorporated information from earlier written or oral sources, like existing poems or historical accounts.*

☐ *The thirty-nine Old Testament books include accounts of events from creation to about 450 years before the birth of Christ. Some debate exists about when some of the books were written, but most scholars agree the majority were written sometime between 1500 and 200 B.C.*

☐ *In addition to the books of the Old Testament, Catholic and Orthodox traditions recognize an additional fourteen books (or portions of books), which often are called the Apocrypha. The majority of these books were written between 200 B.C. and A.D. 100 and focus on events in that period.*

☐ *The twenty-seven books of the New Testament were written in the first century A.D. and include accounts of events surrounding Jesus' life and the establishment of the church, as well as letters of instruction and encouragement from early church leaders.*

 How important do you believe the issue of the trustworthiness of the Bible should be for a person considering the Christian faith? Explain.

Is This Really the Book God Would Have Sent?

I wince to admit this, but it's true. My feelings toward the Bible have often oscillated between adoration and aggravation. I have wrestled with many questions regarding the Bible and still do. One of the most basic has been more of a gut-level objection rather than a scholarly issue. It feels sacrilegious to even voice this question, but sometimes I have wondered if God couldn't have done a better job on the Bible. I mean, if I were God and going to send a book this size to tell all I needed to tell to humanity, is this conglomeration of information what I would have included?

Sometimes it is hard to understand why the Bible spends so much space on extensive genealogies, cryptic stories rooted in historic cultures destined for extinction, and meticulous descriptions of the wealth of kings and the decor of long-gone temples—and then leaves us without definitive statements on important doctrinal issues that have spawned much division in church history. Why so much historically rooted material subject to confusion in later generations? Why a patchwork of history, instruction, poetry, proverbs and prophecy all jumbled together? Why not just clear, concise, chronological instruction with comprehensive coverage of timeless principles in clearly titled and indexed chapters?

When I finally voiced this question to a Christian mentor, I found I was not alone. My mentor admitted she had silently entertained the same question. And since then I've encountered others who have also admitted to wondering the same thing. But I had never heard any Christian speaker or writer address this question until I stumbled onto a short section in Brian McLaren's book *Finding Faith,* which helped me think about this issue in a new light.

McLaren answers these questions by asking another one: if God is having a story unfold in history, how else could it be? Wouldn't it have to come piecemeal from those involved in the events, still too close to have an orderly, distant perspective? And even if God were going to have the accounts edited into a more "acceptable" form, for whom would he edit them: for scientific rationalists or poets, for progressive people or those steeped in traditions, for philosophers or for farmers?

If God wants us to dig deep into his revelation, so it captivates, inspires and transforms us, can we really expect it to be free of challenges and mysteries? If the Bible describes amazing events only experienced a few times in history, can we really expect it to explain these realities in simple, comprehensive language? Would it really be preferable to have a cool reportage of facts and theological discourse? Or would it not be better to see the astonishment, feel the struggle and be continually drawn closer to God in our search for increased understanding?

> Would it really be better for us to have the story rehashed and "sanitized" so we like it more readily and accept it more easily? Or is there some benefit to getting it gritty, breathless, and warm from the lips of those who were there, told in their idioms, through the lenses of their cultures—leaving the job of interpretation and application for our myriad and dynamic settings up to us?
> BRIAN MCLAREN[1]

What are some specific Bible passages or characteristics you have struggled with and why?

Do the insights touched on here help you with these? If so, in what way?

How Do We Know the Right Books Are Included?

A good friend of mine went to college a Christian and came home an agnostic. When we discussed the reasons for her change in view, she said that it was learning in one of her classes that the Bible is just a collection of books arbitrarily chosen by a committee of pompous clergymen that first fueled her doubts about Christianity.

This issue of what books are included in the Bible concerns what scholars call the *canon* of Scripture—its authoritative list of contents. And it is a subject I have sometimes struggled with as well. To be truthful, when looking at some of the people who have risen to authority in the church, I'm not sure I am ready to trust some obscure clergymen who lived hundreds of years ago to tell me what books I should consider divine. But when I look into the subject for myself, this popular theory of the compilation of the Bible doesn't do justice to the whole story.

The Canon of the Old Testament

The Protestant Old Testament includes the same documents as the Hebrew Scriptures. The only difference lies in the arrangement and division of the books. Many of these documents were recognized as authoritative divine revelations very early after they were written. And evidence indicates that rather than being the result of an authoritative pronouncement, the Hebrew canon grew out of a gradual accumulation of these books generally recognized as being inspired.

The details of the timeline are subject to some debate. But all scholars agree that at least the first five books of the Old Testament were fully recognized as Scripture by five hundred years before the birth of Christ, and some believe much earlier. Although many have proposed that some of the other books were added as late as a gathering of Jewish scholars in Jamnia around A.D. 90, evidence suggests that the entire Hebrew canon was well known and accepted much earlier than this.[2]

One strong attestation to this is a passage from the Jewish historian Josephus, written around the same time as the gathering at Jamnia: "We have not tens of thousands of books, discordant and conflicting, but only twenty-two, containing the record of all time, which have been justly believed to be divine. . . . *For though so long a time has now passed*, no one has dared to add anything to them, or take anything away from them, or to alter anything in them" (italics added).[3] Josephus then proceeds to give a summary of these books that appears to indicate the same ones recognized today (although the division and order is different).

The primary basis for the Christian acceptance of the Hebrew Scriptures is Jesus' own attitude toward the Old Testament as seen in the Gospels. From these accounts we find that although Jesus often disagreed with the religious leaders on the meaning of Scripture, he did not disagree with them regarding which books the Hebrew Scriptures should include or the authority they should be given. Additionally, the New Testament writers repeatedly refer to the Hebrew Scriptures as authoritative and inspired.

For me this brought the question of the Old Testament canon down to whether I believed the New Testament is a reliable account of Jesus' life and whether I believed Jesus was who the Gospels claim he was. (These questions are discussed in chapter seven.) If I came to believe these things, my questions about the books of the Old Testament would be largely resolved.

The Old Testament Canon in Jesus' Day

Matthew 23:35 and Luke 11:51. Jesus confirms the Hebrew canon when he tells the Jews they will be responsible for all the righteous blood that has been shed "from the blood of Abel to the blood of Zechariah." Abel is the first martyr recorded in the Hebrew order of the Scriptures and Zechariah is the last.

Luke 24:44. Jesus says, "Everything must be fulfilled that is written about me in the Law of Moses, the Prophets and the Psalms." Many scholars believe he is specifically indicating the three divisions of the complete Hebrew Bible: the Law, the Prophets and the Writings (here probably called the Psalms because it is the first and largest book of the third section).

 Read the following verses and note what they reveal about the views of Jesus and the New Testament writers concerning the Hebrew Scriptures: Matthew 5:17-18; 22:29; Luke 24:25-27, 44; Romans 1:2; 15:4; 2 Peter 1:20-21.

What are your thoughts concerning the Old Testament canon?

The Canon of the New Testament

As with the Old Testament, the formation of the New Testament canon was a gradual process marked by general recognition of the authority and authenticity of books rather than an edict made by one specific council. After Jesus' life, his disciples began spreading the message about his words and deeds, and churches began to spring up throughout Rome and its territories. Originally the disciples' teachings were passed on orally, but after a few decades they began to be written down by the disciples and those closely associated with them.

Modern scholarship confirms that most, if not all, of the New Testament documents were written by the end of the first century. As each document came into existence, it was copied and circulated among the churches. Evidence suggests that the authority the early churches placed on the New Testament derived from the authority of the apostles, whom they believed Jesus had commissioned to carry on his work. The New Testament texts were viewed as being on the same level as the Hebrew Scriptures very early in their existence. This is especially apparent in the fact that in 2 Peter 3:16 Paul's letters are already referred to as "Scriptures," as is Luke's Gospel in 1 Timothy 5:18.

Because of geographic distances, there was sometimes a lag in acceptance of some of the lesser-known books in remote areas. But translations we have from A.D. 170 used by the extreme eastern and western branches of the church indicate general agreement about the canon even in these areas by this time.[4] (They include all the same books we recognize today with the exception of 2 Peter.) The first official churchwide ruling on the canon of the New Testament wasn't until A.D. 397. This ruling confirmed the twenty-seven books already generally recognized.

When I was thinking through these things, the emphasis the church placed on the authority of the apostles made sense to me since their teaching was the closest anyone could hope to get to Jesus' own instruction. It also seemed reasonable to believe that if Jesus really was who he said he was, he would use the church and leaders he commissioned to safeguard a record of his life and teachings for future generations. So I realized that if I concluded the Gospel accounts are a reliable record of Jesus' life and deeds, this would settle many of my questions about the New Testament canon as well.

What are your thoughts concerning the canon of the New Testament?

What About the Apocrypha?

The Old Testament Apocrypha. *Between 300 B.C. and A.D. 100, Jews living in Alexandria, Egypt, completed a Greek translation of the Hebrew Scriptures called the Septuagint. In addition to the recognized Hebrew books, a number of other Jewish documents came to be included in this translation. These additional documents make up what is now commonly called the Apocrypha. Since the Septuagint was the translation used most often by the early church, the debate about whether the Apocrypha should be considered part of Scripture rose early in church history. Although the books of the Apocrypha were well respected among first-century Jews, they were never officially included as part of their Scriptures, and neither Jesus nor any of the New Testament writers refer to these documents as inspired.*

The New Testament Apocrypha. *Additionally, some refer to a number of books that grew up around the New Testament writings as the New Testament Apocrypha. These include a wide assortment of documents, written in the second and third centuries A.D., which claim to be additional gospels and acts and letters of the apostles. In regard to these writings R. K. Harrison explains, "Comparative studies have shown without doubt that the New Testament apocryphal writings preserve at best a series of debased traditions about the Founder and teachings of early Christianity. At worst, the narratives are entirely devoid of historical value and in some respects are totally alien to New Testament spirituality."[5]*

Do Our Bibles Say the Same Thing as the Originals Did?

A few years ago a fellow writer called me, beside himself with frustration. Although an editor's work on a book is usually wonderfully transparent and beneficial, my friend had just received his manuscript back from his publisher and, without permission, the copyeditor had completely rewritten one of the chapters, even including a quote from *herself* under the guise of one of the author's resources.

Although I understood my friend's frustration and agreed the copyeditor had stepped out of line, when I thought about it I could understand the copy-editor's motivation. Have you ever tried to recount a story exactly as it was told to you without adding personal commentary? We humans seem to have an insatiable desire to comment and amend.

This human tendency has sometimes made me wonder if we can really trust our modern Bibles, considering they have been passed down to us through myriad copies and translations. How do we know that scribes before the days of the printing press didn't edit the text or change it to reflect their own theology? How do we know the Bible we have today is not just an obscure reflection of the original?

The Old Testament. When I looked into these questions, I found that belief in the reliability of the Old Testament text is primarily based on three things.

1. The reverence the Jews demonstrated in copying their Scriptures. The Jewish people's attitude toward their Scriptures can be seen in the passage from the Jewish historian Josephus already mentioned, which testifies that "for during so many ages as have already passed, no one has been so bold as either to add anything to [the Scriptures], or take anything from them, or to make any change in them."[6] The Jews held the Hebrew Scriptures in such high regard that a specific class of people developed whose primary responsibility was to preserve and copy the texts. These scribes adhered to an intricate system of rules to ensure accuracy of transmission.[7]

2. The witness of early manuscript families and translations. All manuscripts of the Hebrew Scriptures currently available to us demonstrate widespread agreement regardless of who prepared them or where they were found. This conformity is even present in translations of the text into such diverse languages as Arabic, Latin, Armenian and Greek. If large-scale changes had been gradually introduced into the text, these diverse families of manuscripts separated by years and geographic distance should have revealed them.

3. The confirmation of the Dead Sea Scrolls. The Dead Sea Scrolls are a collection of over eight hundred manuscripts found in the Judean desert in the 1940s, dating back to the second and third century B.C. Before this discovery the earliest copies of the Old Testament we possessed were from around A.D. 900. The Dead Sea discovery afforded scholars a rare opportu-

nity to compare the texts we had with texts a thousand years closer to the originals, taking us back to perhaps within two hundred years of the completion of the youngest book in the Hebrew Bible.

When the texts were compared, the manuscripts gave overwhelming support to the reliability of the textual transmission. As Randall Price, author of *Secrets of the Dead Sea Scrolls,* writes, "We *can* say— and say with greater confidence than ever based on the witness of the Scrolls—that our present text is accurate and reliable, and that nothing affecting the doctrine of the original has been compromised or changed in any way in the manuscript copies."[8]

> Even though the two copies of Isaiah discovered ... were a thousand years earlier than the oldest dated manuscript previously known (A.D. 980), they proved to be word for word identical with our standard Hebrew Bible in more than 95 percent of the text.... The 5 percent of variation consisted chiefly of obvious slips of the pen and variations in spelling.
>
> **GLEASON L. ARCHER**[9]

 Do you believe we have reason to trust that the Old Testament text has faithfully been passed down to us? Why or why not?

The New Testament. Because of the overwhelming number of early copies, translations and quotations we have of the New Testament documents, the case for the reliability of its textual transmission is fairly straightforward. The New Testament was one of the most frequently copied and widely circulated books of antiquity. About six thousand manuscripts of the New Testament or portions of it in its original language are still in existence today and over nineteen thousand copies of early translations—far more than of any other ancient Greek work.

Forty of the Greek manuscripts date back to before A.D. 300, with several dating to the second century—including a portion of John from around A.D. 110. Additionally, nearly the entire text of the New Testament can be reconstructed from quotations in other works from the second and third centuries. Because of this multitude of manuscript evidence, the reliability of today's New Testament text is established on extremely strong grounds.

Do you believe that the textual transmission of the New Testament can be trusted? Why or why not?

Variants. This is not to say that there are not some differences among manuscripts of both Old and New Testament texts. The most common differences involve small unintentional changes such as

☐ confusing letters similar in appearance

☐ writing a word twice or skipping a word

☐ writing a homonym or synonym instead of the original word

☐ misspellings

But some intentional changes can be found in manuscripts as well, such as the following:

☐ revision of grammar and spelling

☐ harmonization of similar passages

☐ elimination of difficult passages

☐ modifications to support a certain theological bent

> At present, we have more than six thousand manuscript copies of the Greek New Testament or portions thereof. No other work of Greek literature can boast of such numbers. . . . Furthermore, it must be said that the amount of time between the original composition and the next surviving manuscript is far less for the New Testament than for any other work in Greek literature.
> PHILIP W. COMFORT[10]

Most variants can be traced back to the original text through manuscript comparison. This leaves relatively few points where scholars have any question regarding which reading represents the original, and in most of these cases the difference in the text is minor. In fact, no significant biblical teaching is affected by any questionable variant. Additionally, most modern study Bibles contain notes that alert readers of any passage in which there is a question.

What are your thoughts on the fact that there are variants among Bible manuscripts?

Examples of Significant Variants

A copy of Samuel found among the Dead Sea Scrolls includes a short passage previous to 1 Samuel 11:1 describing the oppressive deeds of Nahash, king of Ammon.

Among the eight Dead Sea Scroll copies of Jeremiah found, two were made up of a shorter version with some differences in sequence, sentences and names.

In the best Greek manuscripts the Lord's Prayer (Mt 6:13) does not include the words "For yours is the kingdom and the power and the glory forever. Amen."

Mark 16:9-20 is not included in the most reliable manuscripts.

Most early manuscripts do not contain the story of the woman caught in adultery in John 7:53—8:11.

What About the "Proof" That the Bible Is an Unreliable Fraud?

Even knowing all this, sometimes when I go to the library or bookstore I am overwhelmed by the sheer number of books arguing against the reliability of the Bible. At times I wonder if it really is possible that all these people are mistaken. But when I'm feeling like this, it helps to force myself past the sheer numeric intimidation and carefully examine the specific arguments offered. Often when I have done so, I have found the "proofs" in these books manifest some general tendencies that strip them of their power.

Questionable assumptions. Many of these books are based on two questionable assumptions. The first is that all honest scholars came to the conclusion long ago that the Bible cannot be what it claims to be, and the second is that all supernatural knowledge and events are impossible. Many don't even intend their books to provide proof that the Bible is unreliable. They only aim to support their own theory on how the Bible developed, since it obviously can't be a supernatural revelation as it claims.

Undue significance placed on insignificant details. Accepting the assumption that the Bible is not what it claims to be opens the door to a multitude of conjecture. One author argues that the Gospel of Luke was not written by Luke but by a non-Jewish woman far removed from the actual events portrayed.[11] His case is based *solely* on the prominence given Gentiles and women in Luke's Gospel. But who's to say that a Jewish man—perhaps even the doctor we know as Luke—might not be more sympathetic toward women and Gentiles than most in his generation, especially if he was being influenced by God's Spirit?

Unwarranted expectations placed on the text. Why do the Gospels often phrase Jesus' teaching in different words? Why do the details in two accounts of the same incident often differ? Why does the Bible speak of the sun's rising when science has shown that the earth actually moves around the sun? Some critics base their arguments on questions such as these that reflect unjustified expectations. In the days before tape recorders, writers were not expected to concern themselves with exact quotation. It only makes sense that different eyewitnesses would highlight different details when recounting an event. And wouldn't it be expected that the Bible would use the common idioms of the day to communicate?

Overstatement. These books often overstate their case, presenting their material as if there were no evidence to support traditional views of the authorship and dating of the books of the Bible. But this isn't true. Many respected scholars after careful study have reported findings in support of the reliability of the Bible.

Do you agree that the arguments of Bible critics often contain these fallacies? Why or why not?

The Pearl of Great Price

It is not enough, of course, to clear away gut-level objections to the authority of the Bible, understand how it was decided which books to include, investigate the trustworthiness of the text and uncover discrepancies in critics' arguments, although these are important starting points. The real question is whether this book is a divinely inspired revelation to humanity. Some of the Bible critics' arguments are easily dismissed, but others raise tough questions. How can we know this book is from God?

> Again, the kingdom of heaven is like a merchant looking for fine pearls. When he found one of great value, he went away and sold everything he had and bought it.
> MATTHEW 13:45-46

These questions challenged me, even as I was writing this chapter, to consider more seriously than ever why I am willing to base my entire life on this one book. It comes down to five areas of evidence that form the foundation for my reliance on the Bible as God's Word. They can be summarized in the acronym PEARL.

Prophecy. The Bible contains numerous fulfilled prophecies that attest to its supernatural origin.

Experience. In my own life and in the lives of those around me, I have experienced the power and truthfulness of the Bible.

Archaeology. The findings of archaeology have repeatedly substantiated the Bible, attesting to its historical reliability.

Resurrection. When I study the claims for the resurrection of Christ, I find no other explanation for the evidence except that Christ really rose from the dead.

Logic. The Bible offers logically satisfying answers to the questions raised by the nature of humanity and the existence of the world, as no other philosophy I have encountered does.

The previous two chapters discussed the last of these in detail—how the Bible offers satisfactory answers to the questions logic raises about the world around us and about human nature. The next four chapters will discuss the others, beginning with the area that is most convincing to me—the evidence for the resurrection.

If the elements of PEARL can be shown to be true, do you believe this would substantiate the Bible's claims about itself? Why or why not?

If the elements of PEARL are valid, can you think of any reason the Bible shouldn't be considered a trustworthy revelation? Explain.

Digging Deeper

The Canon of Scripture *by F. F. Bruce (Downers Grove, Ill.: InterVarsity Press, 1988). Bruce offers a detailed discussion of the formation of the Old and New Testament canons.*

The Origin of the Bible, *Philip Wesley Comfort, ed. (Wheaton, Ill.: Tyndale House, 1992). This collection of essays serves as a broad introduction to such areas as canon, Apocrypha, authority and inspiration, and reliability of transmission and translation.*

Is the New Testament Reliable? A Look at the Historical Evidence *by Paul Barnett (Downers Grove, Ill.: InterVarsity Press, 1986). An easy-to-read examination of the argument for the reliability of the New Testament.*

Grave Issues

Did Jesus Really Rise from the Dead?

The gospel is the absolute center of the Christian faith. It is also the portion of Christianity that is most readily verified by the evidence. The atoning death, burial, resurrection, appearances, and deity of Jesus Christ are established on extremely strong grounds.

GARY R. HABERMAS, *Dealing with Doubt*

W hen I first began questioning my faith, I remember remarking that if I could just know that Jesus had really lived, I would be satisfied. At that time I naively believed that it was very improbable to establish that an influential Jewish teacher named Jesus ever lived in first-century Palestine. But as I began looking into the evidence for Christianity, I found that the existence of such a person was not often questioned even among those who wished to discredit Christianity. In fact, it was a rather simple task to establish for myself the

Prophecy
Experience
Archaeology
Resurrection
Logic

> And if Christ has not been raised, our preaching is useless and so is your faith. More than that, we are then found to be false witnesses about God, for we have testified about God that he raised Christ from the dead. . . . And if Christ has not been raised, your faith is futile; you are still in your sins. . . . But Christ has indeed been raised from the dead.
>
> 1 CORINTHIANS 15:14-20

existence of this first-century man.

I was wrong, however, in thinking that this minimal fact would satisfy my doubts. It was just the beginning. Establishing that Jesus did exist raised a multitude of other questions about the details and meaning of his life. Were the Gospel accounts of his life reliable? Did he really claim to be God? Was he capable of supernatural acts in support of this claim? Was he crucified by Roman soldiers? And most important, did he rise from the dead, demonstrating his love for me and his power over death?

Looking back I can see how simplistic it was to think that merely establishing Jesus' existence would end my doubts. But at least at that point I had stumbled onto the realization that the truth of Christianity boils down to the truth about a Jewish man named Jesus. If this Jesus rose from the dead, that does much to answer every other question asked in this book, and if he did not, all of the other questions are meaningless.

Have you heard claims that Jesus didn't exist? If so, from whom, and what basis did they offer for this view?

Do you believe that the question of whether Jesus rose from the dead is at the center of arguments for the truth of Christianity? Why or why not?

Did Jesus Really Exist?

John Romer, author of *Testament: The Bible and History*, does not believe that the Bible is divinely inspired or trustworthy in detail. But he has little doubt that a teacher named Jesus walked the hills around the lake called the Sea of Galilee, just as he has little doubt that Alexander the Great truly ruled Greece. He believes both for the same reason—because of the obvious effects their lives had on history. Romer writes:

> Yet this man Jesus lived, of that there can be little doubt. . . . Unlike Alexander, of course, Jesus was a humble man; there are no coins with his face upon them, no contemporary inscriptions telling of his passing. . . . Yet from a village by this lake and from the words of the Gospels came such an

energy, such an effect, that unless the whole movement was a confidence trick of unparalleled dimensions, it is more reasonable to assume that a man called Jesus really lived in Palestine during the Roman Governate.[1]

The effects of Jesus' life can still be seen today, two thousand years after his birth. In fact, every time we glance at the date we are reminded of the impact this man made on countless lives—sufficient impact to convince an entire civilization to renumber its calendar in his honor.

Today Christianity is the most widespread religion in the world, with one in every three people claiming to be a follower of Christ.[2] Churches can be found in every corner of the globe. The life of Jesus has inspired a vast array of art, literature and music. Countless humanitarian ventures have been launched in his name. And this incredible phenomenon can be traced back to first-century Palestine, when the Christian faith suddenly exploded into existence.

Tracing the Timeline

The New Testament establishes the church's birth in the years immediately prior to A.D. 50

The New Testament documents testify to the sudden introduction of a religion based on a man named Jesus. Scholars agree that the earliest New Testament documents were written around A.D. 50.

Suetonius, Roman historian, confirms that in the 50s Christianity newly existed

Writing around A.D. 120 about Nero's reign (54-68), Suetonius states, "Punishment by Nero was inflicted on the Christians, a class of men given to a new and mischievous superstition."[3]

Cornelius Tacitus, Roman historian, confirms details of Jesus' death and that the church existed in A.D. 60s

Writing in 112 about the fire in Rome during Nero's reign (64), Tacitus states:

But not all the relief that could come from man, not all the bounties that the prince could bestow, nor all the atonements which could be presented to the gods, availed to relieve Nero from the infamy of being believed to have ordered the conflagration, the fire of Rome. Hence to suppress the rumor, he falsely charged with the guilt, and punished with the most exquisite tortures, the persons commonly called Christians, who were hated for their enormities. Christus, the founder of the name, was put to death by Pontius Pilate, procurator of Judea in the reign of Tiberius.[4]

Pliny the Younger, governor of Bithynia, confirms the widespread impact of Christianity by A.D. 112

In a letter to the Roman emperor in 112, Pliny, governor of a remote province, asks advice regarding the prosecution of Christians. Even in this remote area at that time, he says, "many of all ages and every rank and also both sexes" were among the Christians, and this new religion was affecting "not cities only, but also the villages and the country." He indicates that Christianity had existed in the region for at least twenty years.

In his letter Pliny gives a glimpse into the lifestyle and beliefs of the Christians of his day by recording their defense to the emperor:

They maintained, however, that the amount of their fault or error had been this, that it was their habit on a fixed day to assemble before daylight and recite by turns a form of words to Christ as to a god; and that they bound themselves with an oath, not for any crime, but not to commit theft or robbery or adultery, not to break their word, and not to deny a deposit when demanded.[5]

 Do you believe adequate evidence exists to establish that an influential teacher named Jesus lived in first-century Palestine? Why or why not?

Are the Gospel Accounts of Jesus True?

Establishing that an influential teacher named Jesus actually lived is still a far cry from establishing whether the Gospels accurately portray the details of this man's life. After all, the Gospels make some pretty unbelievable claims. How do we know that these accounts are true?

When I was struggling with this question, it helped to think through the options of what I could believe about the Gospels. I asked myself, *If the Gospels are not truthful accounts, what else could they be?* I came up with only three possibilities.

1. *Legends spread by those far removed from the events.* Most people who do not believe the Gospel accounts say they are simply a collection

of legends that grew up around the real facts after Jesus' death. This view has become particularly popular in the last two hundred years. It is also the position I was most inclined to believe when I began examining this question.

At the time this view was first introduced, many scholars believed the Gospels were written long after the death of anyone who could have personally witnessed Jesus' words or actions. They theorized that in between the time Jesus lived and the time the Gospels were written, the stories about Jesus had taken on a life of their own and grown to include tall tales of supernatural acts, claims of divinity and an elaborate Easter resurrection story.

But since that time further evidence has surfaced suggesting that the Gospels were written much earlier than these scholars had supposed. In fact, in the 1970s John A. T. Robinson, a renowned Bible scholar who had always accepted the popular opinion of the late date of the New Testament, decided to investigate the evidence for himself. In the process he reversed his former opinion and came to believe that all the New Testament books were written by the early date of A.D. 64. He cited scholarly "sloth," "the tyranny of unexamined assumptions" and "almost willful blindness" for the wide acceptance of the late date theory.[6]

> Arguments that Christianity hatched its Easter myth over a lengthy period of time or that the sources were written many years after the event are simply not factual.
>
> PAUL L. MAIER (professor of ancient history, Western Michigan University)[7]

If Robinson is correct, the time between even the *latest* Gospel and the life of Christ would be around thirty years, not the previous one hundred or more some had believed. And even those who do not agree with Robinson's findings now generally concur that all the Gospels were written *at the very latest* by the end of the first century.

Additionally, the writings of Paul, regarded among the earliest New Testament documents, demonstrate that the elements of the Gospel accounts that skeptics view as most legendary—Jesus' resurrection and claims of divinity—were circulating at least by A.D. 50. A striking example is found in 1 Corinthians 15:3-8:

> For what I received I passed on to you as of first importance: that Christ died for our sins according to the Scriptures, that he was buried, that he was raised

on the third day according to the Scriptures, and that he appeared to Peter, and then to the Twelve. After that, he appeared to more than five hundred of the brothers at the same time, most of whom are still living, though some have fallen asleep. Then he appeared to James, then to all the apostles, and last of all he appeared to me also, as to one abnormally born.

Scholars of all persuasions generally agree that Paul penned these lines around A.D. 55—just some twenty years after Jesus' death.

I was surprised to find such concrete evidence confirming the existence of at least the bare essentials of the Gospel accounts this close to when Jesus actually lived. Most myths the Gospels are compared to have taken centuries to develop—not a mere two decades. Yet I still wondered if it wouldn't be possible for some embellishment to have occurred. But when exploring this option, a few factors spoke strongly against it.

□ As Paul mentions in the passage above, many of the people who played key roles in the Gospel stories were still alive at this time. Paul even indicates he is personally acquainted with many of them.

□ Rather than showing signs of being written by people far removed from the events, some of the historic and geographic details in the Gospel texts reveal the authors were intimately familiar with life in Galilee during the time Jesus lived. As even skeptic John Romer admits, "Indeed, the greater part of [Jesus'] teaching was conducted in three towns so small that they are barely mentioned in texts outside the Gospels themselves. Yet so precise are the Gospels' descriptions of this Galilean landscape that their writers surely knew it well."[8]

> We did not follow cleverly invented stories when we told you about the power and coming of our Lord Jesus Christ, but we were eyewitnesses of his majesty. For he received honor and glory from God the Father when the voice came to him from the Majestic Glory, saying, "This is my Son, whom I love; with him I am well pleased." We ourselves heard this voice that came from heaven when we were with him on the sacred mountain.
> 2 PETER 1:16-18

□ History shows that the very people closest to the events of Jesus' life—Peter, John, James, Thomas and others—were prominent leaders in the early church. For these men the stories of Jesus' supernatural acts, claims of divinity and triumphant resurrection could not be mere hearsay. They would have had to know whether these stories were actually true. And if they were not true, something more than gullibility would have had to be at work.

2. *Lies spread by those involved in the events.* This last insight forced me

to examine a second option. Was it possible that the stories about Jesus' life were outright lies invented by Jesus' disciples? What if the disciples had become so impressed with Jesus' teaching and so attached to the idea of his being the Messiah that they couldn't stand to let go of it even after his death? What if they were so sure Jesus' teaching was the key to peace and happiness for their people that they felt justified in inventing stories that would keep Jesus' message alive?

But I came to believe this was very unlikely, as well, for several reasons.

> A casual reader of the New Testament cannot fail to notice the pains its writers go to in insisting that the revelation in Christ is open to investigation objectively valid.
>
> CLARK H. PINNOCK[9]

☐ History demonstrates that the disciples were beaten, jailed and even executed for their beliefs. Would they have been willing to die for something they knew was a lie?

☐ It is hard to imagine that even a well-meant lie would have motivated the disciples to spread their tale with such breathless enthusiasm as would account for the explosive growth of the early church. Was it really imaginable that absolutely nothing happened on that first Easter morning—that it was only a well-crafted lie that transformed this motley crew of confused individuals into courageous and self-sacrificing missionaries?

☐ Just the mind-boggling number of people who would have had to be involved in the hoax seems implausible—all the disciples, Mary Magdalene, Peter's mother, Joseph of Arimathea, Lazarus, Jesus' family and many others. And all these conspirators would have had to coordinate their stories very soon after Jesus' death while they were still confused and grief-stricken.

☐ Belief in the Gospel stories can be traced back to Galilee and Jerusalem—the very areas in which the events were supposed to have taken place. It is difficult to believe that someone could invent a story that was supposed to have happened in a small rural area and pass it off as truth in that same area within living memory of the residents.

3. *Symbolic stories never claiming to record actual events.* When investigating these first two options, I came across some authors who proposed a third option I had never considered. The Gospel stories of Jesus' life, they claimed, were never intended to communicate actual events but were only symbolic stories invented to illustrate spiritual truths. One advocate of this

view compared the Gospel accounts to Aesop's fables and argued that the point was not whether Jesus actually rose from the dead or performed supernatural acts but that, somehow in some way, early Christians found victory through him. Early Christians, he said, understood that these books were fiction with the purpose of illustrating spiritual concepts, not historical truth.

However, when I read through the New Testament, I couldn't escape the impression that the writers intended to communicate real events open to investigation by their readers. And I saw no evidence in church history to say differently. In fact, the intensity with which these stories were taught, and even the arguments their enemies chose to use against them, strongly suggested the opposite. As Craig Blomberg explains, "At the very least the main outline of the events of Jesus' life, death and resurrection must be historical or the claims of Christianity become incomprehensible. . . . Sceptics down through the ages argued that those beliefs were not true, but seldom did they maintain that those beliefs were not what Scripture was claiming."[10]

 Which of the three alternative views of the gospel listed here do you find most credible and why?

Can you think of any other alternative explanations for the Gospel accounts? If so, describe them and the evidence for and against them.

Do you believe any of these views over the possibility of the Gospels' being trustworthy accounts? Explain.

But Did the Resurrection *Really* Happen?

After considering these options, I found no satisfying explanation for the Gospels except that they are trustworthy accounts of Jesus' life. But I still wondered if it was really possible that Jesus rose from the dead as the Gospels claimed or if there might be some other explanation. Wasn't there another plausible explanation?

Regarding Jesus' crucifixion and empty tomb, even more reasons exist to believe these parts of the Gospel accounts.

☐ Few scholars doubt that Jesus was crucified by Roman soldiers, because it is impossible to believe that anyone would invent such a disgraceful end for their leader. As Romer explains, "The act of Jesus' crucifixion convinces because of its extremely degrading nature. In the Roman Empire crucifixion was a most shameful death. . . . No one but the most bizarre of contemporary theologians would have invented such a miserable ending for the Lord of Heaven."[11]

☐ It also seems unlikely that the Christian community would have invented the story of Jesus' burial in the tomb of Joseph of Arimathea, a prominent citizen and member of the Jewish Council (Mt 27:57-60; Mk 15:43-46; Lk 23:50-53; Jn 19:38-42). Anyone who doubted the story could easily discover whether this important official actually existed and whether he buried Jesus in his own tomb.

> Joseph of Arimathea, a prominent member of the Council, who was himself waiting for the kingdom of God, went boldly to Pilate and asked for Jesus' body.
> MARK 15:43

☐ As for the claim that the tomb was found empty on the third day by a group of women, good reason exists to believe this as well. Since at that time the testimony of women was not respected, it is difficult to imagine that someone inventing this story would choose to have women discover the tomb. The accounts also mention some of the women by name, so it would have been possible to question them. And if the tomb had not been empty, it seems as if the Jewish leaders would have produced the body for all to see if they began hearing stories of Jesus' resurrection.

So if Jesus was crucified and buried in Joseph's tomb and the tomb was found empty, what other possible explanations are there? I could only think of four possible scenarios.

1. *Jesus' body was moved by Jewish leaders.* But why would they do this, especially when it was the very thing they feared the disciples would do (Mt 27:62-64)? And why wouldn't they have produced the body once they realized the confusion moving it had caused? And how do we explain the appearances of Jesus after his death?

2. *Jesus' body was stolen by some of his followers.* But how did they get past the guard (Mt 27:65)? And if his disciples were involved, this brings us back to their dying for a lie. If they weren't involved, who would have taken the body, and is it really feasible that no one would have found out? And this still doesn't explain the appearances of Christ after his death.

3. *The women went to the wrong tomb.* At first this seemed possible to

me. What if the women accidentally went to the wrong tomb and everyone jumped to conclusions? But if the tomb was Joseph's, wouldn't he have been able to quickly correct the mistake? Furthermore, the Gospels say that at least two of the disciples visited the tomb after the women to verify the women's claims. Is it possible that they too went to the same wrong tomb? Additionally, wouldn't the Jewish leaders have produced the body, if they still had it, when the resurrection story began to circulate? And again, what about the appearances?

4. *Jesus survived the crucifixion.* Some propose that perhaps Jesus didn't die on the cross but only fainted and was taken for dead. But is it really possible to believe that he survived being beaten by the soldiers, crucified, pierced through the side with a sword, and then wrapped from head to foot in spice-laden linen? It is difficult to imagine that someone who had been through all of this and had lain in a damp tomb without food or water for thirty-plus hours could unwrap himself, roll away a stone and slip through a Roman guard. Even if this were possible, could this person, weak and in need of medical attention, give his disciples the impression that he was the Prince of Life, the conqueror of death?

 What is your response to these arguments for belief in the resurrection?

The Final Option

In the end none of these other options made sense to me, and I was left with the explanation that the disciples offered so long ago—the one on which they staked their lives. Only the resurrection of Jesus could account for the empty tomb, belief in the resurrection story so soon after Jesus' death, the fervent message of the disciples and the explosive growth of the early church. And only the resurrection could account for the appearances of Christ after his death.

The reports of his appearances were particularly convincing to me. They are present in even the earliest New Testament documents, written when many eyewitnesses were still alive. Jesus appeared to many different people in different locations at different times, and these experiences give no evidence of being some sort of mass hallucination.

On the contrary, the accounts appear to involve distinct events, often happening at unexpected times and witnessed by more than one person. And these appearances didn't come just to those who already believed in Christ. Consider Paul's story. This hard-core Jew encountered the resurrected Jesus while in the process of attempting to stamp out every trace of Christianity. His own words and the profound change in his life testify to the encounter. What else could account for the sudden conversion of this sworn enemy of Christianity?

Even as I write these words, going back over the evidences for Christ's resurrection fills me with hope. It confronts me with the reality of these events. It puts flesh and blood, dust and sweat on the flannelgraph Bible figures I remember from my childhood. It reminds me that when Jesus cried out, "It is finished" (Jn 19:30), his voice was the hoarse voice of a real man giving up his life for me. And when he appeared to his disciples and said, "It is I" (Lk 24:39), it was the very voice of God proclaiming his triumph over sin and death.

 What do you believe the best explanation is for the accounts of the appearances of Christ after his death and why?

 Do you believe Jesus rose from the dead? Why or why not?

Digging Deeper

The Case for Christ *by Lee Strobel (Grand Rapids, Mich.: Zondervan, 1998). This fast-paced book, written by a former legal reporter for the* Chicago Tribune, *examines the evidence supporting the reliability of the Gospel accounts and the resurrection story through interviews with thirteen top experts in various fields and retraces the author's own journey from atheism to faith.*

The Historical Reliability of the Gospels *by Craig Blomberg (Downers Grove, Ill.: InterVarsity Press, 1987). In this comprehensive book, one of America's foremost authorities on the Gospels explores the history of Gospel criticism, tackling questions regarding alleged inconsistencies, the possibility of miracles, the Jesus tradition outside the Gospels, and the trustworthiness of the Gospel accounts.*

Who Moved the Stone? *by Frank Morison (Grand Rapids, Mich.: Zondervan, 1958). When I stumbled onto this little book, I could hardly put it down. Written in the 1930s by a British journalist who began trying to separate legend from truth in the Gospels, this book, which reads like a detective story, follows his journey as he uncovers evidence that leads him to believe in the biggest miracle of all—the resurrection.*

Will the Real Jesus Stand Up? *Paul Copan, ed. (Grand Rapids, Mich.: Baker, 1998). In alternating chapters this book records a debate between a liberal scholar and a conservative scholar on the identity of Jesus and the reality of the resurrection.*

Stones & Scrolls

Does Archaeology Support
the Claims of the Bible?

*We acknowledge a God who heads up history, and as Christians believe,
has even entered into history itself. To see stones which touch this history is
to draw more deeply of the reality of Him who was and is and is to come.*

RANDALL PRICE, *The Stones Cry Out*

I will never forget standing in the musty hallways of the immense tombs
in the Valley of the Kings near Luxor, Egypt. Brightly colored hieroglyphics
surrounded me, showcasing the talent of Egyptian artists
from Old Testament times. Later that day the Egyptian
government announced that in that same valley a hidden
chamber had been discovered containing what some
archaeologists believed might be bodies of the sons of
Pharaoh who were killed during the Egyptian plagues.

If I ever had considered archaeology a dull subject, all

Prophecy
Experience
Archaeology
Resurrection
Logic

such impressions disappeared after the trip Erik and I took to the Middle East. To stand in the Garden of Gethsemane, to touch a wall of the temple in which Jesus and his disciples had worshiped, to see an ancient Egyptian monument that chronicled a battle with the Israelites—all this made the Bible come alive like never before. And reading about the latest archaeological finds was more like piecing together an intriguing mystery than studying a stale history book—a mystery that could bring me closer to answering my questions about the reliability of the Bible.

 What Bible-related archaeological findings are you familiar with? What effect have these had on your faith?

Archaeology and the Bible

Increasing knowledge and opportunity for travel in the early 1800s opened the door to a rich new field of study that focused on unearthing the artifacts of lost civilizations and piecing together the stories they had to tell. These discoveries have clarified, corrected and enlarged our knowledge of human history in ways previously unimagined. Because of this, archaeology offers the person examining the truthfulness of the Bible a rare opportunity to peer into the distant past and compare what is seen with the biblical record.

Cutting Through the Confusion

Yet even if I no longer saw archaeology as boring, I sometimes still found it confusing. For I often stumbled onto *both* sweeping statements by skeptics decrying the historical inaccuracies of the Bible *and* triumphant pronouncements by theologians touting archaeology as one of the "proofs" of the Bible's trustworthiness. My doubts often rose and fell with these archaeological proclamations. Did archaeology really support the claims of the Bible, or did it refute them? And how could equally respected scholars hold such wildly divergent views?

However, as I began examining archaeology more closely, I made some observations that helped dispel some of my confusion.

1. *The kinds of questions archaeology can address.* Some say archaeology "proves" the Bible, but actually archaeology can only address certain types of biblical questions. For instance, archaeology can address the question whether Jericho's walls collapsed, but it cannot prove this was the result of divine intervention. It can address the question whether the Gospels accurately portray first-century Palestine, but it does not easily lend itself to substantiating that Jesus miraculously fed the five thousand. Of course if archaeology repeatedly supports the Bible regarding questions it can address, this lends weight to biblical reliability in other areas as well.

2. *The fragmentary nature of archaeological evidence.* Archaeological evidence is limited to the information that can be collected from the extremely small percentage of artifacts that have survived the centuries *and* have been discovered. As archaeologist Edwin Yamauchi writes, "It would not be exaggerating to point out that what we have is one fraction of a second fraction of a third fraction of a fourth fraction of a fifth fraction of the possible evidence."[1] Because of this, archaeologists often can piece together only a partial picture, and sometimes they assume the picture is complete when in fact a vital piece is still missing.

3. *The subjectivity of conclusions based on archaeological data.* Human interpretation plays a key role in archaeology, and this can't help but be affected by an archaeologist's presuppositions. If an archaeologist begins with the assumption that the Bible is not historically accurate, that person may too quickly dismiss the biblical account. Likewise, an archaeologist who believes in the Bible's accuracy may jump to unwarranted conclusions when an artifact is discovered that has the potential for supporting the Bible. And unlike in other sciences, the conclusions of archaeologists cannot be tested. "Physics and chemistry," Norm Geisler and Ron Brooks explain, "can do all kinds of experiments to recreate the processes they study. . . . Archeologists cannot. They have only the evidence left from the one and only time that that civilization lived."[2]

4. *The tentativeness of archaeological conclusions.* Archaeology is a rapidly changing field. As one museum curator remarked, "Absolute truth in archaeology lasts about 20 years!"[3] Because more archaeological discoveries are being unearthed every day, the archaeological picture is constantly changing, and sometimes long-held conclusions must give way in the face

of new evidence. Because of this, it is wise to keep the whole picture in mind and not jump too quickly between views based solely on one archaeological construct.

 Think of a specific Bible story. What parts of this story could archaeology hope to substantiate, and what parts would be outside its realm?

The Bible and Historical Theories

Understanding these things about archaeology did much to provide me with a frame of reference from which to approach the subject. With these observations in mind I began systematically sorting through some of the archaeological evidence, and as I did, I became increasingly impressed with the archaeological testimony for the Bible's trustworthiness. Despite some outstanding questions, I found that overall archaeology has progressively affirmed the historical and geographical details of the Bible and undermined many of the specific claims of Bible skeptics.

> Has archaeology found nothing to invalidate the claims of the Bible? Nothing. In every single case where the two overlap, the results have been that some biblical claims have been proved, some rendered probable, and none simply disproved by archaeology.
> PETER KREEFT AND RONALD K. TACELLI[4]

Before the days of modern archaeology, it was increasingly common among scholars to regard the Bible as simply a collection of legends divorced from any historical fact, instead of a real historical record of God's interaction with humankind. Many critics confidently cited then-current historical theories as their basis. But as archaeological information has accumulated, it repeatedly has overturned many of the historical theories and substantiated the biblical record.

As archaeologist W. F. Albright explains in *The Archaeology of Palestine:*

> The excessive scepticism shown toward the Bible by important historical schools of the eighteenth and nineteenth centuries, certain phases of which still appear periodically, has been progressively discredited. Discovery after discovery has established the accuracy of innumerable details, and has brought increased recognition to the value of the Bible as a source of history.[5]

Even in several books this size it would be impossible to detail every archaeological finding that is relevant to the Bible, but I have included in this chapter a brief summary of some archaeology findings that shed light on the authenticity of the Old and New Testaments.

Do you find it significant that archaeology has increasingly substantiated historical and geographical details of the Bible and overturned many criticisms against it? Why or why not?

How might this affect the faith a person has in the Bible? How might it affect the faith a person has in current historical theories disagreeing with the Bible?

Examples of Old Testament Discoveries

The world of the patriarchs. The Bible claims that a significant civilization called the Hittites were inhabitants of Canaan when Abraham arrived there. But many early critics doubted that the Hittites ever existed, because no mention of them outside the Bible had ever been found. That was until an archaeological excavation in 1876 unearthed five temples, a fortified citadel and numerous monuments belonging to this lost civilization.[6]

Critics also have dismissed other biblical accounts of the patriarchs, claiming these stories are inventions of nationalistic Jews around 600 B.C. But countless archaeological finds have substantiated the existence of many places and civilizations mentioned in the patriarchal narratives and have confirmed that the cultural practices these narratives depict reflect accurately the time in which the Bible claims they occurred and only that time. It is difficult to explain how storytellers in 600 B.C. would have been able to correctly reflect these details from over a thousand years earlier.

The Jericho conquest. One of the most controversial issues in biblical archaeology is whether the archaeological record supports the biblical account of the conquest of Jericho and other Canaanite cities. In the 1930s John Garstang excavated the site of ancient Jericho and declared that the archaeological findings unanimously supported the biblical record. Evidence showed that the wall of Jericho had in fact fallen outward and that the city had been destroyed by fire around 1400 B.C. just as Joshua 6 maintains.

However, in 1950 Kathleen Kenyon excavated at Jericho and declared that her findings demonstrated that Jericho's destruction occurred in 1550 B.C., far too early to be attributed to the Israelites. Other Canaanite cities showed evidence of massive destruction from 1250 to 1150, too late for the biblical chronology.

But recently Bryant Wood, another archaeologist, has challenged Kenyon's revised dating of the Jericho destruction. Kenyon's dating was based on her failure to find examples of a certain kind of imported pottery that she thought should have been present if the original dating was correct. Wood challenges this by showing the presence of other kinds of pottery that support the original 1400 B.C. date. Wood also points to ceramic figures found in Jericho graves, which form a continuous series from the eighteenth to the fourteenth centuries B.C. And a radiocarbon test was conducted on a piece of charcoal from the final destruction debris, and it yielded a date of 1410 B.C. (plus or minus forty years).[7]

It is interesting to look at all the other details from Jericho that match the biblical record:[8]

☐ The walls of the city collapsed at the time the city was destroyed (Josh 6:20).

☐ The city was destroyed at the spring harvest time, as can be seen by the quantity of grain that was there (Josh 2:6; 3:15; 5:10).

☐ The siege of the city was short, since the grain had not been consumed (Josh 6:15, 20).

☐ The conquerors burned the city (Josh 6:24).

☐ The grain was not plundered as would have been expected from conquerors (Josh 6:17-18).

It has also been argued that the biblical account of the conquest is inaccurate given that evidence of massive destruction exists in other Canaanite cities from around 1200 B.C., too late for the biblical account. But this interpretation overlooks several factors, such as the following:

☐ The Bible readily admits that many Canaanite cities were left unconquered in the time of Joshua (Josh 13:1).

☐ The Bible names only three cities, including Jericho, that the Israelites destroyed in a way that would leave evidence of the destruction, so we should not necessarily expect to find evidence of widespread destruction from 1400 B.C. (Josh 6:24; 8:28; 11:11-13).

☐ Both the biblical record and other archaeological evidence suggest that around 1200 there were several other invading groups, besides the Israelites, who could have been responsible for the destruction of these other cities. In fact, this is the very situation the Bible suggests in the time of the judges, which would align with this chronology.

Hezekiah's reform and victory. The story of Hezekiah is found in 2 Kings 18—20 and 2 Chronicles 29—32. Hezekiah was the son of Ahaz, one of Judah's worst kings. Ahaz worshiped idols and even practiced human sacrifice. But when Hezekiah inherited his father's throne, he determined to rid his country of pagan worship and return to the one true God. He reinstated worship in the Jerusalem temple and destroyed idolatry throughout his country.

In addition to his spiritual reform the biblical record tells that Hezekiah refused to pay the tribute the Assyrians had levied on Judah since the days of his father. For a while his resistance to Assyria was successful and the country enjoyed a time of peace. But in the fourteenth year of his reign Sennacherib, the Assyrian king, retaliated against Hezekiah and attacked Judah with all of the force of his mighty army.

One after another, Judah's cities began to fall to the Assyrians, who were known for their military strength and brutality. As Sennacherib marched toward Jerusalem, Judah's capital, capturing every city in his path, Hezekiah began frantically preparing Jerusalem for the impending battle. His biggest concern was that the city would be cut off from its water supply, which was unprotected outside the city walls. To ensure this didn't happen, the Bible claims, he dug a tunnel to carry water underground directly from the nearby spring into the city. It also says that he fortified the walls of the city and built additional towers and even built a second wall outside the first.

When the city of Lachish, just twenty-five miles from Jerusalem, fell to the Assyrians, Hezekiah made one last attempt to deflect Sennacherib's army by offering a large sum of gold and silver to make up for the tribute he had refused to pay. However, Sennacherib rebuffed his attempt and sent a message to Jerusalem mocking Hezekiah and the God of Judah. In desperation Hezekiah called out to God, asking him to save Jerusalem from destruction.

So what happened? According to 2 Kings 19:35-37:

That night the angel of the LORD went out and put to death a hundred and

eighty-five thousand men in the Assyrian camp. . . . So Sennacherib king of
Assyria broke camp and withdrew. He returned to Nineveh and stayed there.

One day, while he was worshiping in the temple of his god Nisroch, his
sons Adrammelech and Sharezer cut him down with the sword.

This story of how Jerusalem escaped certain capture by the Assyrians is
amazing, and many would undoubtedly question its truthfulness. However,
archaeology has supplied confirmation of many of the details of the biblical
account. The Bible specifically mentions the capture of Lachish by the Assyrians. Remarkably, archaeologists have discovered a ninety-foot mural
depicting this battle between the Assyrians and the people of Lachish in the
palace of King Sennacherib in Nineveh. Excavations from Lachish also
confirm the event.

The water tunnel that Hezekiah dug to prepare for the Assyrian siege can
still be seen today. Even now scientists cannot explain exactly how this
1,750-foot tunnel could have been carved out in limestone without the aid
of compasses or modern tools. Some of the fortifications Hezekiah added to
the city walls also have been discovered as well, including the second wall
he built outside the original one. This outside wall was discovered during an
excavation in Jerusalem conducted from 1969 to 1982. It is called the Broad
Wall because it is twenty-three feet thick. The haste and desperation with
which it was constructed is evidenced by the fact that it was built with stones
from homes of the people. This is alluded to in Isaiah 22:10: "You counted
the buildings in Jerusalem and tore down houses to strengthen the wall."

Archaeology has also confirmed that Sennacherib did not conquer Jerusalem. No reason outside the biblical one given has been found for this
strange turn of events. In fact, after this military campaign Sennacherib never returned to Judah. And a Babylonian inscription has been found confirming that Sennacherib was later killed by his own son just as the Bible says.

Jeremiah's scribe. The book of Jeremiah credits a scribe named Baruch
with playing a significant role in the strategic days before the Babylonian
conquest of 586 B.C. The Bible says Baruch was the personal secretary and
confidant of the prophet Jeremiah. Baruch is even credited with writing
down at least some of Jeremiah's prophecy and going to the temple to read
it when Jeremiah could not go himself.

In 1975 an assortment of clay document seals was found that archaeologists believe date back to the time of Jeremiah and the destruction of the first temple. Written on the clay seals were the names of their ancient owners. Among these was one that bore the inscription of "Berekhahu [Baruch] son of Neriyahu [Neriah] the scribe." Later another seal was found with the name of another scribe mentioned numerous times in Jeremiah, "Gemaryahu [Gemariah] the son of Shephan" (Jer 36:10-12, 25-26). A third name mentioned in Jeremiah was also found: Ishmael, the man Jeremiah says was responsible for the assassination of Gedaliah, the Babylonian-appointed governor (Jer 41:1-3).

Darius and Xerxes. For centuries travelers passing by the Iranian mountain known as the Rock of Behistun couldn't help but notice a huge mural carved into the cliff three hundred feet above their heads. The mural scene includes one man with upraised hands, with ten other men standing in front of him and two behind. No one knew who these men were or how the carving came to be until scholars scaled the side of the cliff and discovered hundreds of wedge-shaped characters that they determined must be an ancient form of writing.

> So Jeremiah called Baruch son of Neriah, and while Jeremiah dictated all the words the LORD had spoken to him, Baruch wrote them on the scroll. Then Jeremiah told Baruch, "I am restricted; I cannot go to the LORD's temple. So you go to the house of the LORD on a day of fasting and read to the people from the scroll the words of the LORD that you wrote as I dictated. Read them to all the people of Judah who come in from their towns."
>
> JEREMIAH 36:4-6

When the writing was finally deciphered, they found one phrase clearly proclaiming, "I am Darius, Great King, King of Kings, the King of Persia." This mural turned out to be the first extrabiblical evidence of the existence of King Darius, named in the Bible as responsible for returning the Jews to Jerusalem and allowing them to rebuild the temple. Also in agreement with the biblical record, a line in the inscription mentioned Darius's son Xerxes, who the Bible names as the king who married Esther.

How do these archaeological finds affect your view of the Old Testament?

Do you know of other archaeological finds that speak to the trustworthiness of the Old Testament? If so, what are they and how have they affected you?

Examples of New Testament Discoveries

Crucifixion techniques. In 1968 the remains of a crucified man from the time of Christ were found in a tomb near Jerusalem. The tomb markings identified the man as Yohanan. The primary evidence of his crucifixion was that his right anklebone was still pierced with a seven-inch-long nail and attached to a piece of wood. Apparently when the man was nailed to the cross, the nail hit a knot and became so lodged that both the nail and the piece of wood remained when the victim was removed.

The discovery of Yohanan refuted two long-held criticisms of the biblical account of Jesus' death. Skeptics had argued that the entire narrative of Jesus' burial in Joseph's tomb was unhistorical because a crucified prisoner would never have been allowed a proper burial but would have been thrown into a common grave reserved for criminals. However, Yohanan's tomb yielded an example of at least one crucified victim who had received a proper burial. Skeptics had also maintained that the Gospels were mistaken in depicting crucified victims as secured to the cross with nails instead of ropes. But the evidence supplied by Yohanan's remains again upheld the Gospel accounts.

The reliability of Luke and Acts. Luke and Acts have come under particular attack by critical scholars. Even today some consider this two-volume work to be a highly fictitious account told by a second-century storyteller far removed from the facts. However, archaeology has repeatedly confirmed the geographical and historical details included in these books.

Luke and Acts mention thirty-two specific countries, fifty-four cities and nine islands without making any mistakes. They even use the correct titles for officials in these varying locations. For instance, the author correctly mentions "politarchs" in Thessalonica, "temple wardens" in Ephesus, "the proconsul" in Cyprus and "the first man of the island" in Malta.

> For Acts the confirmation of historicity is overwhelming. . . . Any attempt to reject its basic historicity must now appear absurd. Roman historians have long taken it for granted.
> A. N. SHERWIN-WHITE (Roman historian)[9]

Skeptics have also repeatedly criticized Luke for certain word choices they believed were inauthentic, but further archaeological discoveries have continually proved the skeptics wrong and the writer of Luke and Acts correct.

James the brother of Jesus. Church history tells us that Jesus' brother

James became a believer after Jesus' death and a leader of the church in Jerusalem. He is mentioned several times in the New Testament (Mt 13:55; Acts 12:17; 15:13; 21:18; 1 Cor 15:7; Gal 1:19; 2:9; Jude 1:1) and is held to be the author of the book that bears his name. An important passage written by Josephus, a Jewish historian, in the early second century confirms this information and tells the circumstances of James's death: "As therefore Ananus was of such a disposition, he thought he had now a good opportunity ... so he assembled a council of judges, and brought before it the brother of Jesus the so-called Christ, whose name was James, together with some others, and having accused them as law-breakers, he delivered them over to be stoned."[10]

Erastus, Corinth's director of public works. In Paul's letter to the Romans written from Corinth, Paul mentions a man named Erastus whom he describes as the "city's director of public works" (Rom 16:23). In excavations of Corinth made in 1929, a pavement was found bearing a Latin inscription that read "Erastus, curator of public buildings, laid this pavement at his own expense." Scholars believe this pavement dates from the first century and the inscription very likely refers to the same man mentioned by Paul.

What is the effect of these archaeological finds on your view of the New Testament?

Do you know of other archaeological finds that speak to the trustworthiness of the New Testament? If so, what are they and how have they affected you?

Ancient Witnesses

While we were in Israel, we visited an archaeological dig in process. The ancient city stretched before us, broken-down walls of white rock tracing the perimeters of homes, shops, stables and public restrooms long deserted. As we walked along, we occasionally found fragments of pottery mixed in with the pebbles under our feet. Our guide explained that these were pieces of ceramic tickets residents had used to gain entrance to the amphitheater. As I held one of them, it struck me that I was holding a ticket someone had used hundreds of years ago—a firsthand witness to the existence and activities of a long-past civilization.

The ancient witnesses of archaeology have made a dynamic contribution to my view of the Bible, giving me a new sense of its historic reliability and reinforcing the credibility of my faith. I wish I had space in this chapter to include even more examples of archaeological discoveries. There are many others pertaining to both significant biblical events and incidental cultural and geographical details.

> **The Bible is supported by archaeological evidence again and again. On the whole, there can be no question that the results of excavation have increased the respect of scholars for the Bible as a collection of historical documents.**
> MILLAR BURROWS (archaeologist)[11]

While archaeology has its limitations and many unanswered questions remain, I came away convinced of one thing. Archaeology has shown the Bible to be much more grounded in history than many people have assumed. Both Old and New Testaments have been shown repeatedly to contain extremely accurate references to the events, customs and geography of the times they describe. "While many have doubted the accuracy of the Bible," Norman Geisler writes, "time and continued research have consistently demonstrated that the Word of God is better informed than its critics."[12]

 What is your response to the statement that archaeology has shown the Bible is much more rooted in history than many believe?

 Do you believe that archaeology generally supports the historical reliability of the Bible? Why or why not?

Digging Deeper

The Stones Cry Out *by Randall Price (Eugene, Ore.: Harvest House, 1997). This is one of the few recent books written for the layperson focusing on archaeological discoveries that confirm the reliability of the Bible.*

Archaeology and the Old Testament *by Alfred J. Hoerth (Grand Rapids, Mich.: Baker, 1998).* Archaeology and the New Testament *by John McRay (Grand Rapids,*

Mich.: Baker, 1991). These two illustrated books, written by top scholars in their fields, offer comprehensive, up-to-date summaries of archaeological findings that relate to the Bible.

What Profit in Prophets

Do the Prophecies in the Bible Really Come True?

If what a prophet proclaims in the name of the LORD does not take place or come true, that is a message the LORD has not spoken.

DEUTERONOMY 18:22

After an event has happened it often seems as if it couldn't have happened in any other way. But sometimes it strikes me how hard it would have been to predict some of the events in recent history a hundred, fifty or even twenty years before the fact. Who could have

Prophecy
Experience
Archaeology
Resurrection
Logic

foretold that a ragtag, disorganized group of British colonists in America would dare to go to war against England and *win?* Who could have guessed that the atomic bomb would be developed just in time to turn the tide of World War II? Who could have foreseen the sudden collapse of communism in the former Soviet Union in the 1990s? So many variables were at play in these events that a difference in any one of them could have thrown the outcome in a completely different direction.

Given this, I often am startled by the way some passages in the Bible seem to mention future predictions as casually as I might throw around details about the recent past. "Wait!" I subconsciously find myself wanting to warn the authors. "Don't you know these predictions will be able to be tested?"

Of course if the Bible is written by frauds as many maintain, someone should have given the authors this caution while they were still alive. *But* if there is an all-knowing God who is behind the writing of the Bible, there is no reason for caution. No risk of being wrong is present for One who knows the future just as surely as the past.

At the mention of Bible prophecy many immediately think of last-days predictions—the stuff of end-time movies, prophecy conferences and even sensationalistic preachers who teach the world is going to end every other Monday. But while the Bible does contain many prophecies about the end of time, it also is generously peppered with numerous other long- and short-term predictions, many of which concern events now in the past.

> Therefore I told you these things long ago; before they happened I announced them to you. . . . You have heard these things; look at them all. Will you not admit them?
> ISAIAH 48:5-6

When I was looking into the claims of Christianity, these prophecies presented another opportunity to test the Bible's trustworthiness. If it can be objectively shown that a specific prediction has passed the point at which it could be fulfilled and has not come true, the Bible itself says this means it is not from God (Deut 18:22). But if it can be demonstrated that the Bible contains numerous specific predictions that have invariably been fulfilled, this yields strong support to the case for its divine inspiration.

Factors Determining the Convincing Value of a Prophecy

☐ *the detail it includes*

☐ *the likelihood of the prophet's being able to guess that the events described would happen*

☐ *the likelihood that the people who knew of the prophecy would be able to fulfill it themselves*

☐ *whether the events that fulfilled the prophecy are known outside the Bible*

□ *whether it can be established that the prophecy was in fact written before the events happened*

In researching Bible prophecy I studied resources from both camps—the camp of those who maintain that the Bible contains many indisputable fulfilled prophecies and those who maintain that many biblical prophecies were obviously never fulfilled and that all the apparently fulfilled prophecies can easily be explained in another way. And although I filled more than seventy pages with notes on biblical prophecies, among the more than 8,352 prophetic verses[1] in the Bible I never found one specific prophecy that I could conclusively show was false, and I found many that uncannily foretold the outcome of numerous future events.

Do you agree that if the Bible could be shown to contain numerous detailed fulfilled prophecies, this would be evidence for the truth of Christianity? Why or why not?

Israel's Incredible History

Remarkable examples of fulfilled prophecy can be seen in the history of the Jewish people still unfolding even today. Over twenty-five hundred years ago the Bible foretold that the Jewish people would encounter war, captivity and exile and that they would cease to exist as a nation and be scattered throughout the world. But it also claimed that despite all this they would continue to survive as a distinct people group and that one day they would be brought back together as a nation in their own homeland. (See Jer 30:1-11; Ezek 37:21-22; Zeph 3:19-20.)

Have you ever heard of a modern-day Philistine, Edomite or Moabite?

I will take the Israelites out of the nations where they have gone. I will gather them from all around and bring them back into their own land.
EZEKIEL 37:21

That's because although these represent great nations in Old Testament times, these people groups, as well as scores of others from that time period, no longer exist. But the Jewish people still *do* exist, against all odds, these thousands of years later, just as the Bible said they would. And they did experience war and captivity, were sent into exile, ceased to be a nation for over eighteen hundred years, and were scattered throughout the world, just as the Bible said they would be. But in 1948, as a result of a series of incredible events, the nation of Israel was reestablished in its ancient homeland.

The Jewish people have been targeted for extinction numerous times throughout history. Even today Israel is surrounded by nations that would like to see it cease to exist. But as Norman Geisler explains, "No other nation in history has managed so successfully to keep a culture, identity, and language intact over hundreds of years, let alone against the genocidal hatred repeatedly encountered by the Jews."[2]

How convincing do you find the prophecies about Israel as evidences for the Bible's inspiration?

The Fate of Other Cities and Nations

The Bible also makes numerous predictions about various other people groups and nations. Skeptics argue that some of these prophecies contain so little detail they could be fulfilled in many ways. However, as I worked through them I was struck by the number of predictions involved and the fact that, regardless of the amount of detail, I found none that could be irrefutably proven false. Without fail the cities and nations the Bible says will be destroyed are destroyed in a way that fits the details of the prophecy, and those the Bible says will continue to exist continue just as foretold.

The prophecies against the city of Tyre are good examples. Tyre was the Phoenician capital and a powerful trading city on the east coast of the Mediterranean. Isaiah 23 predicts that Tyre will be destroyed and then rebuilt. Then Ezekiel, written about one hundred years later, adds that many nations will come against Tyre (Ezek 26:3) including the Babylonians under Nebuchadnezzar (Ezek 26:7). These nations will destroy Tyre, and the rubble of the city will be thrown into the sea, leaving bare rock where fishing nets will be stretched out to dry (Ezek 26:4-5, 12, 14). The passage also foretells that there will come a time when the city of Tyre is no more (Ezek 26:14, 21).

The city of Tyre consisted of a mainland city and an island settlement. Nebuchadnezzar besieged the mainland city in 585 B.C., just as the passage predicts (Ezek 26:8). The city recovered after surrendering to Nebuchadnezzar but was attacked again by Alexander the Great in 332 B.C. Alexander not only attacked the mainland city but also, after destroying it, threw the

| The larger part of the site of the once great city is now bare as the top of a rock—a place where the fishermen that still frequent the spot spread their nets to dry.
PHILIP MYERS (historian)[3] |

rubble from it into the sea, just as the prophecy predicted, to build a bridge for his troops to the island settlement. Today only small fishing towns exist near where the great city of Tyre once stood, and some have commented on the ironic fact that the previous location of mainland Tyre is now used to spread fishing nets to dry.

Read Ezekiel 26. How accurately do you believe the prophecies recorded here describe the history of Tyre? Explain.

The city of Petra is another example. The Bible accurately predicted the destruction of the Edomite cities of which Petra was foremost (Is 34:11-13; Jer 49:17-18; Ezek 25:13). Despite the fact that Petra was ideally situated in a steep mountain valley, making it almost invincible, the city was conquered and deserted just as predicted. In fact, the area was so completely abandoned that no one even remembered the location of this beautiful city, carved into rose-colored valley walls, until it was rediscovered in 1812.

For hundreds of years the magnificent rock houses and buildings of Petra have stood desolate with only desert animals to inhabit them, just as Isaiah predicted:

> Her nobles will have nothing there to be called a kingdom,
>   all her princes will vanish away.
> Thorns will overrun her citadels,
>   nettles and brambles her strongholds.
> She will become a haunt for jackals,
>   a home for owls. (Is 34:12-13)

This prophecy is especially powerful to me, since I was able to visit the site of ancient Petra a few years ago and experience for myself the vast barrenness of this rock-city that formerly was home to thousands.

The Bible includes accurate prophecies about Ammon, Assyria, Egypt, Babylon, Edom, Greece, Moab, Philistia, Phoenicia, Rome, Syria and many other nations.

Do you believe the prophecies concerning these cities and nations support the claim that the Bible is divinely inspired? Why or why not?

The Prophecies of Daniel

Even skeptics admit that if the prophecies in Daniel were actually written around 530 B.C. as the Bible claims, they would indeed be examples of amazing predictive prophecy. Daniel accurately predicts

☐ over six hundred years of world history

☐ the rise to power of the Medes and the Persians, Greece and Rome (chapters 7-8)

☐ the division of Greece into four kingdoms that occurred in 323 B.C. (Dan 8:21-22)

☐ a detailed history of the political intrigues, wars and treaties occurring between 530 and 160 B.C.

☐ the time in which Jesus would live (Dan 9:25)

☐ Jesus' death (Dan 9:26)

☐ the destruction of Jerusalem that occurred in A.D. 70 (Dan 9:26)

☐ the desecration of the temple by Antiochus IV Epiphanes that occurred in 168 B.C. (Dan 11:31)

In fact, Daniel's prophecies so accurately describe future events, and especially those occurring between 530 and 167 B.C., that skeptics maintain they were not written in 530 at all but instead are forgeries written around 167, masquerading historic facts as prophetic predictions.

Read chapters 7, 8 and 11 of Daniel in a Bible with good study notes. Do you think that if these chapters were actually written in 530 B.C., they would be evidence of the Bible's supernatural origin? Why or why not?

The Debate

When I first began studying Daniel, I was surprised both by the detail of Daniel's prophecies and by the number of people who hold the late date theory, speaking of it as if it were an established fact. How could so many accept this theory if it weren't true? I wondered. I was almost afraid to begin looking into the question. Many of my other investigations had seemed to point to the truth of the Bible; would this undermine them? But when I examined the evidence for both sides, I found that the late date theory is not as well established as is commonly assumed, and much evidence actually supports the traditional view.

☐ Both sides recognize that irrefutable evidence points to the existence of the book of Daniel by the middle of the second century B.C. This is why no one claims Daniel was written later than 167 B.C., but even this late date doesn't account for all the fulfilled prophecies in Daniel, some of which were not fulfilled until A.D. 70 (Dan 9:24-26).

☐ To avoid some of the later fulfilled prophecies, skeptics have to maintain that the author of Daniel mistakenly regarded the Medes and the Persians as two distinct empires, making the second and third kingdoms in chapters 2 and 7 represent the Medes and Persians and the last represent Greece, not Rome. But the text indicates that the author viewed the Medes and Persians as one empire (Dan 5:28), as in fact they were. And the symbolism associated with the fourth kingdom seems to point to Rome, not Greece (Dan 2:33; 7:7, 19).

☐ Skeptics assert that since Aramaic didn't replace Hebrew as the language spoken by Jews until much after 530 B.C., the fact that much of Daniel is written in Aramaic reveals it is a forgery. But Aramaic is known to have been spoken in Babylon in 530, and it stands to reason that a Jewish captive living, studying and working in Babylon would also speak Aramaic. Additionally E. Y. Kutscher, a leading Aramaic specialist, has demonstrated that the Aramaic in Daniel is Eastern Aramaic, rather than Western as the late date would require.[4]

☐ Language evidence from the Dead Sea Scrolls demonstrates that the Hebrew and Aramaic of Daniel are from centuries before the time the late date theory would allow.[5]

☐ Skeptics point to the existence of Greek and Persian loan words in the text to support the late date. But only fifteen words of probable Persian influence are used, and since Daniel did serve in the Persian government for several years, his use of such words is understandable. Only three Greek words are used, all names of musical instruments that could have well preceded the 530 date.[6]

☐ Some historical assertions in Daniel have been called into question. But Daniel's accuracy in naming Belshazzar as the last king of Babylon was also ridiculed by Bible critics in previous years, until a new archaeological finding revealed that it was modern historians, not Daniel, who were incorrect. And not only have plausible explanations been offered for all alleged historical inaccuracies in Daniel, but also Daniel includes many unquestionably accurate historical facts, difficult to explain if Daniel were written six hundred years after the events it describes.[7]

What is your response to the debate over when Daniel was written?

Do you think the prophecies of Daniel provide confirmation of the supernatural origin of the Bible? Why or why not?

Messianic Prophecies

A golden strand of hope concerning a future promised son is intricately woven throughout the entire Old Testament. The prophecies concerning this promise begin in broad strokes (Gen 12:3; 49:10), but with each additional revelation the picture becomes more detailed. He will be from the tribe of Judah (Gen 49:10), a descendant of David (Jer 23:5), born in Bethlehem (Mic 5:2), bringing light to Galilee (Is 9:1-2).

Christians believe these messianic prophecies have been supernaturally fulfilled in the life of Jesus and their existence stands as a powerful confirmation of the validity of the Christian faith. But even a casual reading of the New Testament reveals that the Jewish scholars of Jesus' day did not see any evidence of supernatural fulfillment in the events surrounding Jesus' life and that even Jesus' own disciples were often hopelessly confused.

That made me wonder, why, if the Old Testament tells as clearly about Jesus' life and death as Christians say it does, did the Jews—especially Jesus' own disciples—have such trouble recognizing him? Why were they looking for a triumphant military leader rather than a suffering servant? Are the facts of Jesus' life really plainly foretold in the Old Testament, or did Christians just overlay their own beliefs on select texts to force them to say something they do not? To answer these questions, I shut myself away in our guest bedroom one afternoon and began working through the messianic prophecies one by one to see how clearly the picture really points to Jesus.

By the time I was finished, I was elated, and I couldn't wait to tell somebody about what I had found. I was amazed at the detailed portrait of Jesus I read in books written hundreds of years before his birth—including a startling summary of the New Testament plan of salvation, even for Gentiles, and a declaration of the deity and resurrection of Christ. I could think of no natural explanation for these in light of Israel's extreme nationalism, monotheism and loyalty to the old covenant. If the disciples were looking only for a triumphant military leader, it must have been their nationalistic hopes that blinded them to the full implications of these passages—although the prophecies include much talk about how the messiah will bring peace and victory to Israel, they also contain much more.

Job 16:19-21; 19:25-27
He will be an intercessor and mediator for humankind.
He will be a redeemer who will give a ransom for our sins.
He will return to earth in the end times.

Isaiah 9:1-7
He will bring honor to Galilee.
He will be a gift from God born to Israel.
He will bring rejoicing, victory and peace.
This *man* will be rightly called "Mighty God."
He will reign on David's throne forever with justice and righteousness.

Isaiah 42:1-9
He will not just benefit Israel but will also be a light to the Gentiles.
He will be meek and gentle.
A new covenant based on him will bring relief from darkness.

Isaiah 49:5-11
He will be despised and abhorred by the nations before he is recognized.
He will restore Israel.
He will become a light for the Gentiles and bring salvation to the ends of the earth.

Isaiah 52:13—53:12

His appearance will be disfigured and marred, and he will appall many.

He will cleanse many nations, and kings will be overcome because of him.

He will have no beauty or majesty to attract people.

He will be despised and rejected.

He will take up our sins and our sorrows, but we will think he is being punished by God.

He will be pierced for our sins, and his wounds will heal us.

He will not defend himself.

He will die before he has descendants.

He will be buried with the wicked and rich, though he is innocent of all wrong.

He will have life after his death.

By the knowledge of him many will be justified.

> **Surely he took up our infirmities and carried our sorrows. . . .**
> **He was pierced for our transgressions . . .**
> **and by his wounds we are healed. . . .**
> **The LORD has laid on him the iniquity of us all. . . .**
> **For he was cut off from the land of the living;**
> **for the transgression of my people he was stricken.**
> **He was assigned a grave with the wicked,**
> **and with the rich in his death. . . .**
> **After the suffering of his soul, he will see the light of life and be satisfied;**
> **by his knowledge my righteous servant will justify many, and he will bear their iniquities.**
> **ISAIAH 53:4-11**

Micah 5:2-15

He will come from Bethlehem.

He preexisted in ancient times.

He will rule in strength and majesty.

Malachi 3:1-4

He will appear suddenly after a messenger has prepared the way.

His coming will be like a refining fire.

The Time of the Messiah

   Daniel 9:24-26 is the only Old Testament passage that pinpoints the exact time when the Messiah would come. It can seem confusing with all its "sevens," but it is definitely worth taking the time to understand. The sevens in this passage are generally understood to refer to sets of seven years. That means seventy sevens would be 490 years. Take a minute and note the six specific things this passage says will happen during those years.

   The text goes on to reveal that it will be seven sevens plus sixty-two sevens until the long-awaited ruler comes. How many years would that be? What does the passage say will happen then? What will mark the beginning of this time period?

Cyrus made a decree to rebuild the Jerusalem temple in 538 B.C., which was reiterated later by Darius, but this doesn't mention rebuilding the city (2 Chron 36:20-23; Ezra 1:1-4; 6:1-5). Artaxerxes I authorized Ezra to return to Jerusalem in 458 B.C. to reinstate worship (Ezra 7:11-26). But it was not until 444 that he issued the decree recorded in Nehemiah 2:1-8, which specifically mentions rebuilding the city.

Incredibly, if we take into account that many scholars believe the ancient Jewish calendar was based on a 360-day year rather than our 365 days and do the math in reference to the decree that specifically mentions rebuilding the city, we arrive at March 30, A.D. 33, the exact date commonly accepted for Jesus' triumphant entry into Jerusalem.

Some dispute the basis for the 360-day reckoning of the Jewish year and the exact date of Jesus' triumphant entry. Others argue that Daniel's years should be viewed as only a round number. But even when these arguments are taken into consideration, the time frame still falls within the lifetime of Jesus!

Since looking into the messianic prophecies for myself, I have become convinced that they stand together as persuasive evidence for the truth of Christianity. When examined closely, even some of the most surprising parts of the gospel story can be found tucked away in the dusty pages of these ancient Jewish Scriptures. Despite the obvious nationalism of the Israelites, the prophecies declare that the Messiah will bring salvation to the Gentiles. Despite the extreme monotheism of Judaism, the prophecies hint at the fact that this man will possess deity and be the Son of God. And despite the obvious preposterous implications, the prophecies clearly state that this triumphant, all-powerful ruler will be executed for our sins.

What do you think about the messianic prophecies of the Bible? Which, if any, do you find particularly convincing?
Do you think the messianic prophecies confirm the supernatural origin of the Bible? Explain.

A League of Its Own

Michelle, a fifteen-year-old girl I know, calls the horoscope hotline every morning, anxious to hear predictions about her day. One morning the hotline gave her very specific information. It told her to be careful with her money because someone would try to take advantage of her that day. She went through the entire day carefully watching her allowance. By nightfall she was deeply disappointed because she hadn't come across any instance when anyone even *could have* taken advantage of her. Despite the number of people today claiming to be able to predict future events, it seems foretelling the future is no easy task.

> The year 1999, seven months,
> From the sky will come a great King of Terror.
> NOSTRADAMUS (sixteenth-century seer)[8]

When investigating the prophecies of the Bible, I was surprised to find that none of the books that other religions consider holy seem to contain prophecies like it. A full 27 percent of the Bible's text is prophetic material. Though some other holy books do contain some predictions, the prophecies of the Bible seem to be unique in number, detail and fulfillment.

The Bible's prophecies also seem to stand out among the predictions of modern psychics and astrologers. When reading books containing prophecies of Nostradamus, Mother Shipton, Edgar Cayce and others, I was struck by how cryptic and vague many of them are; even followers of these seers often have to admit that many of the most specific prophecies did not come true.

> I make known the end from the beginning, from ancient times, what is still to come. I say: My purpose will stand, and I will do all that I please.
> ISAIAH 46:10

The same appears to be true for present-day psychics. In fact, in a study performed by *The People's Almanac*, out of seventy-two predictions of twenty-five top psychics, sixty-six were not fulfilled.[9] This 8 percent success rate falls far below the 100-percent fulfillment standard the Bible sets for itself. As Henry Morris writes, "No man or angel or demon can predict specific events and personages that will appear scores or even hundreds of years in the future. Only God can do this. . . . Consequently, it is in His Word . . . and only there, that prophecies of this sort are found."[10]

Are there any Bible prophecies that you believe can be proved false? If so, explain.

What is your view of predictions from sources other than the Bible?

How do you think these prophecies compare to those of the Bible?

Do you believe that the fulfilled prophecies in the Bible substantiate its claims of divine origin? Why or why not?

Digging Deeper

Encyclopedia of Biblical Prophecy *by J. Barton Payne (Grand Rapids, Mich.: Baker, 1973). This comprehensive book includes a discussion of every prediction in the Bible and helpful tables that list prophecies by subject for easy reference.*

The Messiah in the Old Testament *by Walter C. Kaiser Jr. (Grand Rapids, Mich.: Zondervan, 1995). Working through the entire Old Testament, Kaiser examines all the direct messianic prophecies and explores their development and meaning.*

Testing the Track Record

Does Christianity Really Make a Difference in People's Lives?

I have come that they may have life, and that they may have it more abundantly.

JOHN 10:10 (NKJV)

Carol was a fellow student in a graduate English course. Although I never spoke to her personally, a comment she made in class has reverberated through my mind many times. Our class was discussing a self-discovery book that was part of the required reading. Making reference to Native Americans, the author stated that all those looking for spiritual fulfillment must begin with the religion of their own ancestors.

Prophecy
Experience
Archaeology
Resurrection
Logic

The class was debating this statement when Carol spoke up with a passion that seemed to betray an inner conflict far beyond the scope of our simple discussion: "But how is that possible," she asked, "when Christianity, the religion of *my* ancestors, has brought nothing but hatred, hypocrisy and division?"

Have you heard people make these kinds of accusations against Christianity? If so, when and what did they say?

What has been your response to these assertions?

Is Christianity Really a Curse?

The Bible promises that following Christ will bring personal peace, brotherly love, true fulfillment and victory over evil. If we could see this demonstrated in real life, it would be powerful evidence for the truth of Christianity. But the popular perception today is that not only does the Christian faith not have a *positive* impact, it actually has a *negative* one. One of my professors once even called Christianity "the curse of Western civilization." Carol's question poignantly expresses a common reason why many dismiss Christianity without a thought and others begin to doubt its truthfulness: the track record of Christians.

The wife of a leading youth pastor in my childhood denomination ran off with the father of one of the students. A widower who attended our church committed suicide, leaving his bewildered teenage daughter as his sole survivor. Another church member was convicted of sexually molesting his stepdaughter. A prominent pastor in our town was arrested for using his own church to launder drug money.

These examples and others, just from my own experience, cast an ominous shadow. Newspapers and history books are full of even more accounts, including a nauseating variety of scandals, hypocrisy and hate crimes stretching back to the Inquisitions and Crusades of the Middle Ages and beyond—all done by people claiming the name of Christ. Do these examples truly represent the effects of Christianity on the world? Or does Christianity actually transform lives for the better as the Bible claims?

Look up John 14:27, John 13:35, John 10:10 and Titus 2:11-14; note the promises about the effects of Christianity.

What experiences have you had with Christians that have made you question the truthfulness of Christianity?

The Christianity of the Bible

A new command I give you: Love one another. As I have loved you, so you must love one another. By this all men will know that you are my disciples, if you love one another. (Jn 13:34-35)

Be devoted to one another in brotherly love. Honor one another above yourselves. . . . Be joyful in hope, patient in affliction, faithful in prayer. Share with God's people who are in need. . . . Bless those who persecute you; bless and do not curse. Rejoice with those who rejoice; mourn with those who mourn. Live in harmony with one another. Do not be proud, but be willing to associate with people of low position. Do not be conceited. (Rom 12:10-16)

But the fruit of the Spirit is love, joy, peace, patience, kindness, goodness, faithfulness, gentleness and self-control. (Gal 5:22-23)

Will the Real Christians Please Stand Up?

To begin answering these questions for myself, I had to think through what it means to be a Christian—and what it does not mean. Christ himself said that many will call themselves Christians who are not. In Matthew 7:22-23, he says, "Many will say to me on that day, 'Lord, Lord, did we not prophesy in your name, and in your name drive out demons and perform many miracles?' Then I will tell them plainly, 'I never knew you. Away from me, you evildoers!' "

According to this, being a Christian is more than calling yourself a Christian, holding a position in the church or claiming to do something in Jesus' name. And as I thought about it, that made sense, considering many insincere reasons exist why people might choose to call themselves Christians:

☐ because they want to feel included in a group

☐ because of the expectations of parents, friends or employers

☐ because it gives them an opportunity to hold a position of honor or importance

In other passages Jesus plainly states what it does mean to be a Christian. It means believing in him and obeying his teaching (Jn 3:16-21; 8:31). As I read such passages, it struck me that all the evils committed in the name of

Just as we would not discard liberty because people abuse it, nor patriotism, nor courage, nor reason, speech, and memory—though all abused—no more should we eliminate true religion because self-seekers perverted it.
WILLIAM WILBERFORCE
(British statesman and abolitionist)[1]

Christianity do not only go against our own ethical standards but are contrary to the teaching of the founder of Christianity—Christ himself.

Unfortunately, selfish and insincere people can pervert all good things, and all positions of authority or influence can be abused. So it stands to reason that all evils done in the name of Christianity were not necessarily done by Christians. As D. James Kennedy notes, "Some people have called themselves 'Christians' who have lived in total opposition to the principles and teachings of the Master from Nazareth."[2]

What do you think it means to be a Christian and why?

What is your response to the statement that all the evils done in the name of Christianity may not have been committed by Christians?

Read Matthew 13:24-39. How might this passage relate to this discussion?

The Life and Times of the Inquisitions and Crusades

When the balance of power shifts to the church, as it did in the Middle Ages, it becomes extraordinarily advantageous to call yourself a Christian, regardless of your true beliefs. At the time of the Inquisitions and Crusades, the church had become the ruling authority of the land, and church officials possessed unprecedented power and wealth. This would invariably draw to the church self-seeking, power-hungry people, many of whom were not even Christians. These people would begin filling both the pews and the pulpits and helping determine the future direction of the church.

But Can All "Christian" Evils Be Explained This Way?

Although the existence of insincere people who call themselves Christians can account for *some* of the evil done in the name of Christianity, this unfortunately cannot account for all of it. After all, I consider myself a sincere Christian, but I know I have done many things unworthy of that name.

I discovered that it is important to understand, though, that the Bible never claims that the moment people accept Christ they no longer will do anything wrong. In fact, the New Testament is full of examples of Christians acting in very unchristian ways. Instead the Bible teaches that when persons become Christians, they begin a refining process toward becoming a perfect reflection of Jesus' holiness, compassion and wisdom. But the process lasts an entire lifetime, and throughout the process the Christian is always allowed the choice of whether to take the next step.

The Christians we encounter every day are at different points in this refinement process. And the Bible is clear that Christianity welcomes all people, not just those who are already considered "upstanding" or "respectable." Some, from a human standpoint, may have further to go in the refinement of their behavior than others when they decide to follow Christ. As C. S. Lewis explains in *Mere Christianity*, we cannot judge the effects of Christianity by whether all Christians are better than all non-Christians. We must judge by whether a *specific* Christian is a better person with Christ than *that* person would have been without him.[3]

I look at my own life. I have mentioned some examples of unchristian behavior I've seen in the lives of professing Christians, but I could have filled the same sentences with examples of unchristian things *I* have done. What about my own egotism, self-absorption, deceitfulness and immorality? I have done many things that I would never want associated with Christ, but I didn't do them *because* of my Christianity but *in spite of it*. And to whatever extent I integrate Jesus' teaching into my life, it begins to transform me into something better than I am.

> Such a history is marked by the folly and wickedness of leading Christians on almost every page, but I came to realize, in studying the account, that men have done evil not because of their Christianity but despite it—that Christianity has been not the source of, but the supreme (often the sole) restraining factor on, mankind's capacity for wrong-doing.
> PAUL JOHNSON
> (historian)[4]

Look up Matthew 26:69-74, Luke 9:46 and 1 Corinthians 5:1. Note the behavior described. Do you think the people involved were Christians? If so, what does this imply?

Would you say Christianity has made you a better or worse person? Explain.

The Rest of the Story

Many wrongs have been done in the name of Christianity, but this is by far not the end of the story. As D. James Kennedy writes, "The Church has never been perfect. Far from it. But the *total* record should be examined. In doing so, the good far, far outweighs the bad."⁵

Despite popular opinion to the contrary, it can be seen throughout history that Christian principles have radically changed society wherever they have been accepted, and that Christians have often been at the forefront of social reform and benevolent endeavors. Here are just a few examples:

☐ In ancient Greece and Rome it was common for parents at all social levels to abandon unwanted or imperfect children to be eaten by wild animals or starved. It was the Christians who established orphanages to care for these abandoned children and in the end stopped this practice of child abandonment through swaying public opinion and encouraging new laws.⁶

☐ In the Middle Ages it was the church that educated the masses and established the first universities. Even today, many of the world's greatest universities can be traced back to Christian origins. In the last two hundred years Christians have been the primary force in bringing education to millions of people in Third World countries.⁷

☐ During the Middle Ages it was the church that founded the first hospitals. And Christianity is directly responsible for the establishment of such people-helping organizations today as the Salvation Army, the YMCA, World Vision, Compassion International and myriad others. In fact, "more hospitals, orphanages, rest homes, and rescue missions have been dedicated to [Jesus] than to all other religious leaders combined. More people-helping efforts have been founded, financed, and perpetuated by His followers than all others."⁸

☐ The New Testament has sometimes been criticized for not directly forbidding slavery. However, Paul's calling a slave "a brother beloved" (Philem 16 KJV) was absolutely revolutionary in his day. Further, the New Testament principles of unconditional love and respect for all humanity (1 Cor 12:13; Eph 6:8; Col 3:11) set the stage for the elimination of slavery. And although some Christians supported slavery, many others led the way to its abolishment in both ancient and recent times. Two-thirds of the members of the U.S. abolition society in 1835 were ministers. Abraham

Lincoln's writings are peppered with biblical quotes, and many of the "engineers" in the Underground Railroad were Quakers.[9]

☐ Christians were often at the forefront of efforts to improve treatment of women in the world. William Carey, a missionary to India, fought for years to bring an end to the custom of burning widows on the funeral fires of their husbands. Amy Carmichael, another missionary to India, committed herself to rescuing girls who were raised to be temple prostitutes. And the American crusade for women's voting and property rights in the 1800s was largely made up of evangelical Christians.[10]

☐ The New Testament's insistence that women are equal heirs of God's grace and that husbands should treat their wives with respect, understanding and sacrificial love (Gal 3:26-28; Eph 5:25; 1 Pet 3:7) was also a revolutionary concept in its day. Although Christianity has often been criticized for suppressing women, the countries most affected by Christianity are generally the ones in which women enjoy the most respect. In many non-Western cultures today women are still denied education, forced to do the majority of the work and considered their husband's property.

> In particular, respect for the dignity and responsibility of the individual has been a feature of our society which stems directly from Christian teaching and has been worked out in terms of universal suffrage, universal education and individual liberty.
> FREDERICK CATHERWOOD (former British industrial adviser)[11]

 Do you agree that Christianity has had these positive influences on society? Why or why not?

Changing the World One Person at a Time

In addition to all the social reforms and benevolent endeavors Christianity has fueled, Christianity has positively affected countless millions of individual lives. I heard a story of a Christian speaker who was interrupted during his presentation by a skeptic who protested, "Atheism has done more for the world than Christianity!"

The speaker replied with a challenge: "Tomorrow night bring a hundred people whose lives have been changed for the better by atheism, and I'll bring a hundred whose lives have been changed for the better by Christ."

According to the story, the skeptic was never heard from again.

I don't know if this story is true, but I have never forgotten it. It brings to my mind the faces of many people who have told me—some with tears in their eyes—how Christ has transformed their lives. Just among people I have met, I could easily gather a hundred and more who would enthusiastically come to testify how they have experienced the power of Christ.

Tom's story. "I enjoyed killing people and was good at it," Tom admitted to me. Tom had grown up an abused child, consumed by hatred for his father. As far back as he could remember, he never had turned away from a fight; he always reveled in opportunities to hurt others. When the Vietnam War broke out, Tom enthusiastically joined the Marines and was assigned to an assassination squad. This finally gave him the opportunity to act out his hatred without fear of punishment, and he unleashed all his rage on the Viet Cong. Although he was wounded several times and given permission to go home, he fought to stay.

When he finally was sent back to the United States, he arrived a bitter alcoholic. He married and divorced twice within five years and found he was a dismal failure at being a husband and dad. That was when Tom met Christ. He says the moment he determined to follow Christ, it felt as if a physical weight lifted from his shoulders.

Since that day his life has changed drastically. He was able to forgive his dad and leave the hatred and violence behind. He was able to marry and become a responsible father and husband, and he has devoted his life now to helping others rather than hurting them. Tom is an elder in my church and is very honest about where he has come from. But I cannot see one trace of that angry, violent alcoholic in the man I now know.

Eva's story.[12] If you met Eva today, you would see a short, jolly redheaded woman with dark eyes and dimples, who still claims to be thirty-nine. But the story she has to tell will take your breath away. She was a Jewish girl in Nazi Germany. When she was ten years old, as she was walking to visit her grandparents, she was captured by Nazi soldiers and placed in a concentration camp. There she was physically and psychologically abused and used in various medical experiments. Once she was forced to stand on her toes in the sewer for days just because she had smiled at someone as she walked across the camp. Another day she was beaten unconscious by soldiers at an ammunition factory where she was forced to work.

At sixteen Eva was among those freed when the Allied forces won the war. On her release she found that almost all of her family had been slaughtered at other concentration camps. Eva mistakenly believed that the Nazis, as Gentiles, represented Christianity, and she came to bitterly hate anything that had to do with Christians or Christ.

Years later, however, Eva's own daughter became a Christian. When this happened Eva felt so betrayed she threw her daughter out of her home. Later Eva's husband also became a Christian. Finally Eva prayed, "God, if it is true that Jesus is the one, then I will accept it and do whatever you want me to do."

Today Eva is a Christian speaker who travels around telling others of the power of Jesus' love. When she speaks of her captors she speaks with love and forgiveness and even prays for their salvation. Although her memories are still painful, from personal experience she is able to say, "Jesus can give you the inner strength for healing and forgiveness if you want it."

Mani's story. "Demons are real," Mani says. He knows from experience. Mani grew up in the jungles of the northern Philippines, where the most powerful woman in his village was the witch doctor who communicated with the spirit world. Mani says he himself saw the witch doctor possessed by demons. The demons always demanded sacrifices, but they were never satisfied.

Then one day a missionary walked into their village and told them of a God who had created the world and was stronger than all the demons. Mani eagerly read a copy of the Gospel of Mark that the missionary had translated into his language. When he came to the account of the crucifixion, he threw the book to the ground. Why did this God allow his Son to die? Didn't he have the power to save him? Mani didn't want a powerless God; surely this God was weaker than the demons because he couldn't even save his own Son. But as Mani turned to walk away, he felt the Spirit of God speak to his heart, saying, "I did it for you."

Mani eagerly accepted this God into his life, but by then the missionary was gone from his village. Mani didn't have the money to leave his village and go to one of the Christian schools he had heard about, and he had no way to learn more about his new God. In desperation he prayed, "I want to know you more; please give me a way." To his great excitement, a short time later the missionary unexpectedly returned. He said he was looking for a Filipino to help him with Bible translation, and he wondered if Mani would be interested—the only stipulation was that the missionary board wanted to send him to Bible college.

Do you know people whose lives have drastically changed for the better because of Christianity? If so, what is their story?

Pale Reflections

These are just three people who have experienced the changing power of Christ in their lives. I have found churches and history books filled with countless others—people like Augustine, a fourth-century playboy; John Newton, a slave trader; Chief Tariri, a jungle headhunter; C. S. Lewis, an Oxford intellectual; Chuck Colson, a member of Nixon's special counsel. These and so many more stand as evidence of the truth of Christianity demonstrated through its life-changing power.

> In the end historical facts and logical rules must be assimilated into and validated by the lived world; conclusive evidence is always experiential. Scripture is clear both that Christianity involves doctrine and that it is a way of living that verifies that doctrine.
> WILLIAM DYRNESS[13]

In fact, this has become one of the evidences of Christianity that I rely on most when I find myself struggling with doubt—because it is evidence that I have experienced firsthand, not only in the lives of people around me but also in my own life. I have personally experienced God's presence leading and comforting me and his power exposing my pride, uncovering my apathy and refining me into something better than I am.

Questions like the one Carol asked plus many of my own have caused me to look more deeply into the impact of Christianity. And although I often am discouraged by inconsistencies and failures I see among Christians, myself included, I have become increasingly convinced that Christianity does have a radically positive impact on people's lives. People I have met who truly appear to know Christ and sincerely try to live according to his teaching do demonstrate a vibrant reality. Although they may bear little resemblance to the perfect image of

Christ, when you look closely, you can see the beginning of a pale reflection.

 Have you experienced the power of Christianity firsthand? Explain.

How convincing do you believe the evidence from Christianity's track record is in confirming its validity and why?

 Do you agree that Christianity makes a positive difference in people's lives as it promises and that this is further evidence of its truthfulness? Why or why not?

This concludes the chapters dealing with the evidences for Christianity summarized in "PEARL." In the next three we will explore three common barriers to belief—the claims of science, the existence of evil and the prevalence of other religions.

Digging Deeper

What If Jesus Had Never Been Born? *by D. James Kennedy and Jerry Newcombe (Nashville: Thomas Nelson, 1994). This book explores the impact Christianity has had on humanity in areas such as civil liberties, medicine, the arts, economics, sexuality, education and morality.*

Great Conversions *by Frederick S. Leahy (Belfast, North Ireland: Ambassador, 1998). This little book tells the story of twenty-eight lives transformed by Christ.*

God Beyond the Telescope

But What About Science?

Science without religion is lame,
religion without science is blind.

ALBERT EINSTEIN, *Out of My Later Years*

Of all my science teachers I remember Mr. Boline most vividly. He was fairly young, tall and thin. He invariably wore cowboy boots and a long, full mustache, which made him look more like Wild Bill Hickok than a typical high school biology teacher, but perhaps that was why some of us liked him more than we typically liked science teachers.

Although most of what Mr. Boline taught in his class made sense to me, occasionally some things he taught conflicted with what I had been told by my parents and church. Of course this wasn't the first time I had encountered such contradictions, but it was the first time I remember caring enough to think about them much. When I questioned Mr. Boline, he was pretty patient with me, but after a while he became incredulous that I would continue to question "established science" in favor of "religious myths."

College brought more science teachers and classes, and by this time I had quit asking questions. I had learned to live a double life, giving one set of answers to my science teachers and another set to my Sunday school teachers. But my questions still persisted. I couldn't help coming away from my science classes with the distinct notion that my teachers believed science had disproved God and religion once and for all, and a growing part of me wondered if they were right.

For some modern science stands as a daunting barrier to faith, while others don't find the chasm between science and faith difficult to span at all. Where are you in this spectrum and why? Are there any specific scientific issues that make you question Christianity? If so, what are they?

Are Science and Religion Fundamentally at Odds?

After the impression I had received in school, I was surprised to learn that the Christian belief in a rational God who created rational beings in a rational universe had played an important role in the rise of modern science. The ancient world viewed nature as being under the control of various unpredictable gods and thus erratic and incomprehensible. Only after the Christian belief in one transcendent, unchanging Creator God helped replace this view did people begin to see the universe as based on rational, knowable laws and as worthy of being studied.

In fact many of the pioneers of science were ardent Christians. Francis Bacon (1561-1626), credited with developing the scientific method, wrote, "There are two books laid before us to study, to prevent our falling into error; first, the volume of the Scriptures, which reveal the will of God; then the volume of the Creatures, which express His power."[1] And Johannes Kepler (1571-1630), considered the father of modern astronomy, described science as "thinking God's thoughts after him."[2]

These pioneers of science did not see any fundamental conflict between science and religion. However, some today maintain that such a conflict does exist. Some of these people even define science in such a way that it excludes the possibility of the supernatural. But on close inspection this view often can be traced to a confusion of the terms *naturalism* and *science*.

 Do you think religion and science are fundamentally opposed? Why or why not?

A Sampling of Scientists Who Believed

Robert Boyle (1627-1691), founder of modern chemistry, was a well-known Christian who wrote and translated religious works and founded the Boyle Lectures, a lecture series with the purpose of convincing people of the truth of the Christian faith.[3]

Galileo Galilei (1594-1642), although well known for his confrontation with the church, was a man of faith. He wrote in a letter, "Holy Scripture could never lie or err, but its decrees are absolute and inviolable truth. . . . Although Scripture can indeed not err, nevertheless some of its interpreters and expositors may sometimes err."[4]

Isaac Newton (1642-1727), English mathematician and physicist, professed faith in Christ. He said, "I have a foundational belief in the Bible as the Word of God, written by men who were inspired. I study the Bible daily."[5]

Blaise Pascal (1623-1662), pioneer in mathematics and probability science, wrote a number of religious books expressing his faith and urging others to turn to Christianity.[6]

Naturalism Versus Science

While science could be defined as the observation and experimental investigation of the natural world, naturalism is a philosophical worldview shared by some but not all modern scientists. The basic presupposition of naturalism is that nothing exists outside the material world—that is, we and everything around us can be explained by natural laws and processes. In this view science is usually considered the sole source of true knowledge, and anything that cannot be verified by the scientific method is considered suspect. However, here are some important factors to note about naturalism.

☐ The truth of naturalism *itself* cannot be proved scientifically.

☐ As discussed in chapter four, many recent scientific discoveries are pointing to the possibility of God, and as discussed in chapter five, many aspects of our own nature and experience cannot be explained in terms of naturalism, including the *very belief in naturalism.*

☐ Though naturalism usually views things that cannot be verified by the scientific method as invalid, many important things that shouldn't be dismissed do not fit into this category—such as love, courage, mercy and purpose.

What evidence can you think of to support belief in naturalism? Do you believe things must be scientifically provable to be valid? Why or why not?

Are Science and Religion Mutually Exclusive?

Some attempt to evade the discrepancies between religion and science by saying that science and religion have nothing to do with each other. Or as a statement from the National Academy of Sciences reads, "Religion and science are separate and mutually exclusive realms of human thought."[7] The problem with this is that most of us find day to day that science and religion do overlap and that what we believe scientifically does affect what we believe regarding religion. For example, I have found that I cannot hold as scientific fact that as leading scientist George Gaylord Simpson claimed, "man is the result of a purposeless and natural process that did not have him in mind"[8] and simultaneously believe that God created human beings in his own image.

Science and Christianity

But even many who would say that science isn't *fundamentally* at odds with religion still maintain that the findings of science have disproved religion, and specifically Christianity. This widely accepted view has caused many Christians to stumble and countless seekers to dismiss Christianity without further thought. Is it true that science has rendered Christianity obsolete? Those who answer yes to

> A little science estranges a man from God. A lot of science brings him back.
> FRANCIS BACON (father of the scientific method)[9]

this question generally point to two specific areas in support of their answer: evolution and miracles.

Have you heard people claim science disproves Christianity? What examples have they given?

Do you believe that science and religion are "mutually exclusive realms of human thought" that have no bearing on each other? Why or why not?

Has the Theory of Evolution Disproved Genesis?

A few weeks ago I was flipping through the television channels and stumbled onto a debate about evolution in a popular sitcom. The stereotypical blond girl who obviously had more beauty than brilliance offhandedly mentions to her friends, one of whom is a scientist, that she doesn't believe in evolution. The scientist, shocked, tries desperately to convince her of her error. She dismisses each of his arguments with a shrug of her shoulders and a collection of outrageous counterarguments. "But evolution is a scientific fact!" the scientist finally sputters. "How can you not believe it?"

I would guess that this episode left more than one Christian with the same unsettled feeling they often experienced in high school science classes. Evolution is the hot spot people usually think of first when discussing Christianity and science, and many have been taught that the theory of evolution has disproved the Bible once and for all. But, is this true? And what does it mean when someone says that the theory of evolution is a scientific fact?

Has the theory of evolution affected your view of Christianity? If so, in what way?

The Three Definitions of Evolution

When I was looking into this issue, I quickly realized that the answers to such questions depend heavily on how the term *evolution* is defined. People usually mean one of three things when using the term.

1. When most people speak of evolution, they are referring to the theory

that all life evolved from the simplest organism *through purely natural processes* with no conscious purpose.

2. But *evolution* can also refer to any kind of large-scale change *without* the restriction that only natural processes were involved.

3. And *evolution* can also refer to relatively minor developments among animals in one species.

The least controversial of the three usages is of course the third one, which is sometimes called *microevolution*. Microevolution asserts that over time, through processes such as natural selection, gene mutations and hybridization, new varieties of species are formed. However, microevolution does not involve large-scale changes through which a species could move to a higher classification. In other words, it doesn't allow for a monkey to turn into a human being or a small land mammal into a whale. The occurrence of microevolution is well documented, and most Christian scholars agree that microevolution does not contradict biblical teaching in any way.

The first five chapters of Charles Darwin's *On the Origin of Species* (1859) dealt with this concept of small-scale evolution through natural selection, which was in itself a groundbreaking theory. But in the rest of the book he theorized that the processes at work in microevolution could progress without limit and account for all the variety of life that exists today. Since such large-scale evolution would take millions of years to occur, it is obviously not directly observable.

Many unresolved problems still exist with this theory. And despite evolution's widespread acceptance today, many respected scientists—some of whom have no religious reasons to oppose evolution—still have serious questions about the reality of large-scale evolution.

With that said, it is also important to mention that Christians have vary-

> For Darwin, all evolution was merely an extension of microevolutionary processes. Yet despite . . . the reality of microevolution, not all biologists have shared Darwin's confidence and accepted that the major divisions in nature could have been crossed by the same simple sorts of processes. . . . The German zoologist Bernhard Rensch was able to provide a long list of leading authorities who have been inclined to the view that macroevolution cannot be explained in terms of microevolutionary processes, or any other currently known mechanism. These dissenters cannot be dismissed as cranks, creationists, or vitalists, for among their ranks are many first rate biologists.
> MICHAEL DENTON (molecular biologist)[10]

ing views on the issue of large-scale evolution, with some believing that the creation "days" of Genesis correspond to long geological ages in which God used evolutionary processes to bring about life. When these people speak of evolution, they are talking about it in the second sense listed above: large-scale evolution that does not exclude the possibility of the supernatural.

Of course the most controversial of all the definitions is the first one—naturalistic evolution. Many use the three senses of the word interchangeably and assume that because evolution in one sense may be well supported scientifically, all three types of evolution are proven facts. However, even if large-scale evolution is accepted as true, it is beyond the scope of science today to say that this process occurred without any intervention by a supernatural power or that no supernatural power exists. When the renowned scientist Carl Sagan said, "The cosmos is all that is or ever was or ever will be,"[11] he was stating a personal belief that is far beyond the limits of any known science.

Do you believe in evolution in any of these three senses? Explain. What is your response to the claim that naturalistic evolution has not been proved?

What are your thoughts about the other two senses of evolution? Do you think they contradict the Bible? Why or why not?

Digging Deeper

Darwin on Trial *by Phillip Johnson (Downers Grove, Ill.: InterVarsity Press, 1993). Johnson offers a comprehensive summary of arguments against large-scale evolution and naturalism.*

Evolution: A Theory in Crisis *by Michael Denton (Bethesda, Md.: Adler & Adler, 1986). A molecular biologist gives a thorough presentation of the purely scientific arguments against large-scale evolution.*

Three Views on Creation and Evolution, *J. P. Moreland and John Mark Reynolds, eds. (Grand Rapids, Mich.: Zondervan, 1999). This is a good resource if you are interested in learning more about the spectrum of theistic thought concerning evolution. It contains sections written by proponents of the three dominant views: young-earth creationism, old-earth creationism and theistic evolution.*

Are the Miracles in the Bible Scientifically Possible?

The second perceived contradiction between Christianity and science concerns the issue of miracles. Yesterday I fell into conversation with a retired geologist who believes that Jesus was a good moral teacher but most of what the Gospels say about him is pure invention. I asked him what he based his opinion on, and he was quick to answer. He said he didn't believe the Gospel accounts because of all the miracles they contain. As a scientist, he didn't believe things happen without a scientific cause. "I haven't seen a miracle happen today," he stated, "and I find it hard to believe they ever happened."

From Noah's flood to walking on water to the resurrection story, the Bible is full of miraculous tales. And this geologist is not alone in finding these miracles cause for doubting the truth of Christianity. Can a sane person in this scientific age actually believe in miracles?

 Have the miracles in the Bible caused you to question its reliability? Why or why not?

Are there some miracles in the Bible that you find easier to accept than others? If so, which ones, and why do you think this is?

A Double Order of Christianity—Hold the Miracles

Some have tried to sidestep the issue of the miraculous by attempting to extract miracles from Christian teaching. These people claim that all the miracles in the Bible are simply mythological stories that the biblical writers used to represent spiritual—not historical—truth. When I first encountered this argument, it seemed an appealing possibility—a way to keep all the relevance of Christianity while doing away with the troublesome problem of having to believe the miraculous.

But when I tried to reorganize my thinking about Christianity accordingly and subtracted all the miraculous, I was left with a confusing muddle of high-minded thoughts that had lost all their power. If the New Testament was saying anything, it seemed to be saying that we can have a new relationship with God through the significance of Jesus' life. But if Jesus was just a person like me who died and was buried just as I will be, on what basis is this new relationship offered?

I came to find that I agreed with C. S. Lewis who wrote, "[Christianity] is precisely the story of a great Miracle. A naturalistic Christianity leaves out all that is specifically Christian."[12] In fact, when attempting to identify the purely symbolic meanings of the miraculous stories in the Bible, I realized that to maintain the stories have any meaning at all, the very least I could come away with was that a powerful God, who created nature and loves us, does exist and is intensely interested in our lives. And with that in mind, it made no sense to believe that such a God would *not* at times supernaturally intervene in the events of history.

 Do you agree that even if taken metaphorically, the miracle stories of the Bible seem to teach the existence of a powerful God, who created nature, loves us and is intensely interested in our lives? Why or why not?

If such a God exists, do you think it is more difficult to believe that this God would or would not intervene in human affairs? Explain.

Modernist theologians ... claim that it is of no religious importance whether Moses really led Israel through the Red Sea or whether Jesus' body was really resurrected; the religious question is whether Israel saw God's hand in their history, and whether "Easter faith" was resurrected in the hearts of the disciples. But this seems ridiculous and self-contradictory; it implies that God really led Israel by not really leading it, and that there was an "Easter faith" without an Easter.
PETER KREEFT AND
RONALD K. TACELLI[13]

Science and Miracles

So if Christianity cannot be divorced from the miraculous, that leaves us right back where we started, asking if science has disproved miracles. But if an all-powerful God *does* exist, is there any scientific reason to doubt the possibility that this Being's acts might at times deviate from the normal course of nature? Those that would answer yes to this question often point to one of three reasons.

1. *Miracles contradict natural laws.* Many who disbelieve in the miraculous claim that what we have discovered about natural laws excludes the possibility of miracles. But natural laws are only a description of how nature normally functions, and belief in miracles does not deny that nature *normally* functions in these set ways. In fact, it is necessary to recognize the existence of natural laws before one can

even speak of miracles. Miracles, by definition, are exceptions to these laws. Discovering these laws can do nothing to tell us whether or not a miracle is possible.

2. *Nothing happens without a scientific cause.* This argument is an example of confusing naturalism with science. It is naturalism, the philosophy that nothing exists outside of the material world, that leads to this belief, not science. Nothing in science can prove that everything always has a scientific cause.

3. *Science has never documented a miracle.* Some would say that even though science may not *prove* everything has a scientific cause, it has given us ample reason to believe this because science has never documented a miracle. However, the scientific method can study only those things that *normally* occur in nature and are *repeatable*, and a miracle is an isolated event that is not, humanly speaking, repeatable. Therefore a miracle is outside the realm of scientific experimentation. With that said, it is also interesting that science has documented many things that it cannot currently explain. It is our *faith in science* that makes us identify these things as unexplained phenomena rather than miracles.

> When a thing professes from the very outset to be a unique invasion of Nature by something from outside, increasing knowledge of Nature can never make it either more or less credible than it was at the beginning. In this sense it is mere confusion of thought to suppose that advancing science has made it harder for us to accept miracles. We always knew they were contrary to the natural course of events; we know still that if there is something beyond Nature, they are possible.
> C. S. LEWIS[14]

Can you think of any other scientific argument against miracles? If so, explain.

So Why Haven't We Seen Any Miracles?

Beyond all this I suspect that the major reason most of us have trouble believing in miracles is that we *personally* have never experienced an obvious miracle. This is true for me. Although I have experienced some events that were uncanny in their timing and details, I have never seen anything that defied all attempts of a natural explanation. So if miracles are real, why don't we see obvious miracles around us everyday?

1. *Because an obvious miracle,* by definition, *must be rare.* As I state that I have never experienced an obvious miracle, I have to admit that I'm not sure what I would call an obvious miracle. Would I need to see for myself someone walking on water or turning water into wine? With my skeptical mind and the proliferation of Vegas-style magicians, I'm not sure even these things would convince me. And these kinds of obvious miracles, by definition, must be rare. If each of us had had the opportunity to walk on water, this would no longer be an obvious miracle; it would just be an unusual mode of transportation.

> [If God's reality] were too obvious, then even the most selfish, meanspirited person would believe in him and even (for selfish reasons) try to serve him. . . . There is good reason to think, then, that God would give people "room" to reject him, because he only wants people to believe in him who are willing to believe in him.
> C. STEPHEN EVANS (Christian philosopher)[15]

2. *Because miracles most often are performed at great spiritually significant moments in history.* The Bible doesn't promise that miracles will be experienced equally in all times. As Lewis explains, "God does not shake miracles into Nature at random as if from a pepper-caster. They come on great occasions: they are found at the great ganglions of history—not of political or social history, but of that spiritual history which cannot be fully known by men."[16]

3. *Because of our unbelief.* The Bible indicates that unbelief prevents miracles (Mt 13:58). I daresay that many in our scientific age likely would not believe in a miracle even if they saw one, just like the rich man's brothers in Luke 16:31.

4. *Because God doesn't coerce faith.* The Bible indicates that God wants us to serve him voluntarily. I believe if we were truly confronted with the overwhelming power of God through his *repeated* and *obvious* interference in the world, there would be no room for voluntary love; we would all be overwhelmed into submission.

If an all-powerful Creator exists, do you believe there is any scientific reason to doubt that miracles may occur? Explain.
Do you believe science is able to say undeniably that no higher power exists? Why or why not?

Digging Deeper

Miracles: How God Intervenes in Nature and Human Affairs *by C. S. Lewis (New York: Macmillan, 1960). I drew much for this section from this book. It is somewhat tedious to read, especially at the beginning, but offers wonderful mind-stretching insights.*

In Defense of Miracles, *Douglas R. Geivett and Gary R. Habermas, eds. (Downers Grove, Ill.: InterVarsity Press, 1997). This thorough book offers discussions on the possibility of miracles from philosophical, scientific and historical points of views.*

The Limitations of Science

When I began looking into science and religion, I was surprised to find that it is not even *possible* for any known science to disprove God. It is *naturalism*, not science, that eliminates the possibility of the supernatural. If an all-powerful God does exist, then accepting the acts of miracles and creation is not difficult. Additionally, even macro-evolution, the one area people point to most to disprove Christianity, has not itself been proved; even if it were, this would still not address whether the process might not have been accomplished by a Creator.

> Faith tells us what the senses cannot, but it is not contrary to their findings. It simply transcends, without contradicting them.
> BLAISE PASCAL (inventor, scientist, mathematician)[17]

But even with a thorough understanding of these points, perceived contradictions between religion and science are unavoidable. As Norman Geisler explains, "Biblical theology involves human understanding of the biblical text. As such, it is subject to misunderstanding and error. Likewise, science is fallible human attempts at understanding the universe. So conflict is inevitable."[18] This conflict can be especially difficult for Christians involved in science.

A friend who was a biology major particularly struggled with this. Raised in a Christian home, he was overwhelmed by the underlying thought systems in his science courses that challenged many of the things he had been raised to believe. He began questioning his faith and searching for his own answers. "It was a scary time for me," he says, "a faith-shaking time." For him, however, it came down to gaining a clearer understanding of the limitations of science. "Science looks for patterns," he explained, "and measures things, but they haven't come up with a God-meter yet."

 Do you believe science has disproved Christianity? Why or why not?

Contending with a Tragic World

But What About Evil?

The persistence of evil is an inescapable fact of human history. In the experience of evil and reflection upon it, mankind reaches the extreme limit—the decisive question of the meaning of life, of the sense and nonsense of reality. Therefore, the Christian view of human existence faces its most serious test when applied to the presence of evil in the world.

MICHAEL PETERSON, *Evil and the Christian God*

A carjacker steals a woman's car while her six-year-old son is still in the backseat. The terrified mother flings open the back door and frantically attempts to rescue her son. But her little boy's foot becomes tangled in his seatbelt, and the carjacker speeds off, dragging the boy to his death.

Early one morning a youth group from a small church sets out, full of excitement, for a day at an amusement park. Just before arriving, their van collides with a semi-trailer. The twenty-nine-year-old youth pastor and five of the kids are killed instantly.

A little girl is born into the home of an abusive alcoholic father. Not long after birth the doctors discover she has a rare skin disease that makes her hands and feet blister painfully. Her father tells her she is ugly and no one will ever love her. But she overcomes all this and grows up to marry a wonderful man. They begin a home together and are just starting to talk about having a child when she suddenly begins to lose her eyesight and the strength in some of her limbs. At twenty-six she is diagnosed with multiple sclerosis of the most aggressive kind and is told by the time she is thirty she may be blind and confined to a wheelchair.

Some Christians may claim that such tragedies do not shake their faith in the least, but I cannot say this. Sometimes it feels as if my faith evaporates in an instant, like a drop of water in a burst of heat, when I encounter such things. Of all the questions I have had about my faith, this is among those I struggle with most. Why do such senseless things happen? Where is God in these situations?

 Have you encountered tragedies that have shaken your faith? Explain.

The Inescapable Question

People throughout recorded history have struggled with the existence of evil and suffering. Wherever humans can be found an almost universal cry of protest against the cold facts of reality arises. Why do babies die? Why do innocent people suffer? Why are we able to hurt one another so badly? Why do some starve while others have plenty of food? Even the coldest heart cries out in pain when tragedy strikes near enough. Something deep inside us demands that any religion that claims to be true would surely have to give a satisfying answer to such questions.

Some maintain that the very existence of such evils as holocausts, wars, rapes, murders, diseases, earthquakes, plane crashes and even the more common heartbreaks and injustices we suffer every day should be enough to silence any argument for the truth of Christianity. For these people not only does Christianity with its all-powerful, all-loving, all-just God lack satisfying answers, but it makes the problem even more difficult. Somehow it is easier to accept that there is no God than that God would exist and allow such atrocities.

In the past when my heart has been torn with doubt, I have had similar thoughts. But at other times, when I have been able to get past the pat answers many Christians throw around in times of suffering, I have caught a glimpse of a solid reality that finally begins to make real sense of the seemingly senseless question of the existence of evil. And the key to beginning to see this reality seems to lie in beginning to understand the nature of love.

 Have you heard people denounce Christianity because of the existence of evil in the world? If so, in what circumstances?

The Choice in Love
"What is love?" I sat in a restaurant with Erik on a chilly day a few months before we became engaged, discussing this very question. We were considering the possibility of getting married but were both struggling with the enormity of such a decision. How could we know that we were the right ones for each other? It kept circling back around to our love for each other, but when we tried to say exactly what that meant, the concept seemed surprisingly out of reach.

Love is one of the most real things I have ever experienced, yet it seems to be one of the hardest concepts to pin down. The joy of laying my head on Erik's shoulder, of receiving a card with heartfelt words from my mother, of seeing my dad's eyes tear up when I give him a kiss, of hearing my little boy giggle when I hold him close—these things seem to lie beyond the scope of analysis. But despite its incomprehensibility, most would agree love is incomparably priceless. In fact, most of us would never want to live in a world where love is not possible.

When you think about it, though, love is meaningful only when it is freely given. If someone had been holding a gun to Erik's head forcing him to marry me, his wedding vows would have been less than romantic. And the only thing that makes a kind action kind is that the person performing the action was not required to do it. It is not particularly kind of me to pay my taxes, since if I didn't the IRS would confiscate my house and throw me in jail. It *would* be kind of me, however, if I decided to give a homeless person the same amount of money I pay in taxes each year.

True love or kindness always involves some sort of choice. The less someone is required or expected to do an action, the more loving or kind the action is considered. And for a person to really have a choice, it must be truly possible for that person to choose something else. That means for true love to be possible, individuals have to have the capability to choose the opposite.

This brings us to a strange paradox. The very choice that makes such wonderful experiences as love, kindness, courage and self-sacrifice possible is also the very choice that makes hate, selfishness, cowardliness and cruelty possible.

 What is your response to the claim that love always involves a choice?

But If God Can Do All Things ...

One of the essential beliefs of Christianity is that God can do all things. Luke 1:37 clearly states that "nothing is impossible with God." So, many ask, if God is all-powerful, why couldn't he have created a world in which love and kindness were not dependent on also being able to choose the opposite?

> It is no more possible for God than for the weakest of His creatures to carry out both of two mutually exclusive alternatives; not because His power meets an obstacle, but because nonsense remains nonsense even when we talk it about God.
> C. S. LEWIS[1]

I think the answer to this question can be found by examining what it means to say God is all-powerful. When we say this, we are stating a belief that nothing that exists poses any threat or obstacle to God. We are *not* saying that he can do something that is self-contradictory. A self-contradictory statement is nonsense. It is like trying to say God could have made a world where one equals two. The very definition of *one* excludes the possibility of its being two.

In the same way, in the very essence of love is the concept of choice. It might be possible for there to be something that looks like love that does not involve a choice, but it would not be love in the sense that we know it. A sophisticated robot could theoretically mimic every loving action and word available to humans, but it would not be love.

 Do you agree that God's omnipotence wouldn't allow him to do two contradictory things? Why or why not?

What do you think about the idea that creating love without a choice would be self-contradictory?

But Why So Much Evil?

When I began to understand the necessity of choice in love, it helped me see the existence of evil and suffering in a new light. But the question why *so much* evil exists still remained. Why is it that good and evil don't seem to have a level playing field? Why does it take so much effort to be truly good and loving while selfishness comes without trying? Why would God have created a world like that?

Of course the Bible teaches that God did *not* create a world like that. When God created the world, everything in his creation, including humanity, was completely good. However, one of the good things he created was our ability to love him and each other, but by the very nature of love this also included the possibility of choosing not to love.

The Bible says God created us in his image to have a relationship with him. On every page of the Bible is the awe-inspiring message of God's love for us and desire for us to return this love. But because of the nature of true love, if we are to be capable of really loving God, we have to be left free to make the choice. And if we are truly free to make the choice, the possibility must exist that we will choose *not* to love God.

> Good seems like delicate china: precious but fragile. Evil seems like a bull in a china shop: strong and triumphantly destructive.
> PETER KREEFT AND RONALD K. TACELLI[2]

Nearly everyone in the Western world knows the story of Adam and Eve's disobedience, perhaps almost too well. We have heard it both preached and ridiculed as the subject of high-minded sermons and low-minded jokes. But perhaps the Genesis account deserves a closer look.

When I am considering the account of the Fall, it helps to remember that there is more to the story than is written. The story clearly does not include the kind of detail we expect from modern journalism, and this is understandable when we consider that this bare-bones account was passed down from prehistoric times to speak to humans in every stage of civilization.

C. S. Lewis pictures one scenario of the way things may have been at the time of the Fall. He envisions that the perfect consciousness given to the first humans "ruled and illuminated" their whole being, "flooding every part of it with light."

> Man was then all consciousness. . . . His organic processes obeyed the law of his own will, not the law of nature. His organs sent up appetites to the judgement seat of will not because they had to, but because he chose. Sleep meant to him not the stupor which we undergo, but willed and conscious repose. . . . Wholly commanding himself, he commanded all lower lives with which he came into contact. . . . However rich and varied man's experience of his fellows (or fellow) in charity and friendship and sexual love, or of the beasts, or of the surrounding world . . . God came first in his love and in his thought, and that without painful effort. In perfect cyclic movement, being, power and joy descended from God to man in the form of gift and returned from man to God in the form of obedient love and ecstatic adoration.[3]

The simple fact is that in wanting to be what man as a creature could not be, man lost what he could be. In every area and relationship men have lost what finite man could be in his proper place.
FRANCIS SCHAEFFER[4]

Whether or not this is exactly the way things were before the Fall, the Bible teaches that the first humans were in close communion with God and living peacefully in an essentially good world. Then they chose to disobey God. This act had dire consequences, separating humanity from God and plunging the world into its current fallen state. In this act Adam and Eve chose selfishness over love for God. They turned away from God and made themselves their own idols, fixing their natural inclinations on themselves rather than on God.

 What is your response to the account of the Fall?

The Consequences of the Fall
The Bible is clear that the consequences of Adam and Eve's sin were widespread. Somehow that one decision cast the whole course of humanity

and the world in a new direction. This can be seen in the pronouncements God makes when he confronts Adam and Eve with their sin in Genesis 3, and it is echoed throughout Scripture. The choice of sin introduced death into the world (1 Cor 15:22), and humanity's relationship with God was changed for all time. Our natural inclinations became selfish, as Romans 5:19 says: "Through the disobedience of the one man the many were made sinners."

> Thus all day long, and all the days of our life, we are sliding, slipping, falling away—as if God were, to our present consciousness, a smooth inclined plane on which there is no resting.
>
> C. S. Lewis[5]

But this is not all. In the Genesis account and throughout Scripture we see that the natural order of the world changed as a consequence of humanity's sin. Without giving more detail, Genesis speaks of the introduction of a cursed earth, painful toil and thorns and thistles, and Romans 8:20-23 says that "creation was subjected to frustration" and that it is "groaning" as it waits to be "liberated from its bondage to decay" through the redemption of humankind. This seems to indicate that the Fall brought not only the prevalence of moral evil—those evils that are direct results of selfish human choices—but also the existence of natural evil—evils like diseases, earthquakes and accidents.

I have asked myself if it was fair for God to attach such heavy consequences to one choice. But then I began to see that this wasn't some small, incidental choice. It was a choice about whether humanity would serve God or serve self, and human beings chose self. We do not know but that the consequences were just the natural outpouring of that choice. Peter Kreeft and Ronald K. Tacelli in *Handbook of Christian Apologetics* explain it in this way:

> To help understand Creation and the Fall, the image of three iron rings suspended from a magnet is helpful. The magnet symbolizes God; the first ring, the soul; the middle ring, the body; and the bottom ring, nature. As long as the soul stays in touch with God, the magnetic life keeps flowing through the whole chain, from divine life to soul life, body life and nature life. The three rings stay harmonized, united, magnetized. But when the soul freely declares its independence from God, when the first iron ring separates from the magnet, the inevitable consequence is that the whole chain of rings is demagnetized and falls apart. When the soul is separated from God, the body is separated from the soul—that is, it dies—and also from nature—that is, it suffers.[6]

We also might ask why God didn't just reverse these enormous consequences of the Fall by some sort of miracle. However, if God had stepped in and erased the consequences of Adam and Eve's choice, it would not have been a real choice. "It would, no doubt, have been possible," Lewis writes, "for God to remove by miracle the results of the first sin committed by a human being; but this would not have been much good unless He was prepared to remove the results of the second sin, and of the third, and so on forever."[7] A world in which humanity knew by experience that God would always erase the consequences of any bad choice would be a world in which true choice was not possible.

Read Genesis 3:14-24, and list the consequences mentioned there of Adam and Eve's sin.

What do you think about the fact that God attached such enormous consequences to this choice?

What is your response to the idea that God could have miraculously reversed these consequences?

So Why Create at All?

Sometimes I have wished for oblivion. Sometimes the world seems so oppressive and difficult and humanity so capable of suffering that it's easy to wonder if it would not have been better if God had not created at all. At such times I have asked why, if God is all-wise, he chose to create the world knowing the hatred, terror, starvation, slaughter and agonizing grief that would result.

But I suspect this is an entirely emotional question, not a rational one. It is more of an expression of my temporary loss of hope than a true assessment of reality. For what does it mean to say it would be better for nothing to have existed? Better for whom? How can anyone gain anything by not existing? And who can put a value on one happy heart, the joy of falling in love, the wonder in experiencing a sunset, or the possibility of true communion with the God?

Have you ever wondered why God would create at all? If so, in what circumstances?

What are your thoughts about this question?

Redeeming Evil

No discussion of the Fall, though, is complete without a discussion of redemption. Though God might have been perfectly justified in leaving things as they were after the Fall, he chose not to do that. God, through Jesus, became human and subjected himself to the effects of evil in order to restore our relationship with him. As Philippians 2:6-8 says, Christ, "being in very nature God, . . . made himself nothing, taking the very nature of a servant, being made in human likeness. And being found in appearance as a man, he humbled himself and became obedient to death—even death on a cross!"

Somehow, in the same way Adam and Eve's sin gave us death, Jesus' death gave us life. The Bible says that all evil will ultimately be defeated through what Jesus did on the cross. Ironically, the evil choices of people played a key role in the events that led up to Jesus' crucifixion. God used the very existence of evil to bring about its destruction.

> For just as through disobedience of the one man the many were made sinners, so also through the obedience of the one man the many will be made righteous.
> ROMANS 5:19

Amazingly, when we reflect on it, we can see other ways that God uses evil to defeat itself and bring about good. As Joseph said to his brothers, "You intended to harm me, but God intended it for good" (Gen 50:20). This doesn't diminish the abhorrence we should have for evil. The Bible says God hates evil, and God's use of evil for good in our lives usually depends on our own hatred of it. But realizing this does deepen our appreciation of God. Consider the ways God uses evil for good.

☐ It is in times of pain that we most often turn to God. As Lewis writes, "God whispers to us in our pleasures, speaks in our conscience, but shouts in our pains: it is His megaphone to rouse a deaf world."[8]

☐ Tragedy is often what binds hearts together, forces people to overcome differences and causes individuals to truly appreciate each other.

☐ The existence of evil in our world gives us the greatest opportunity to build moral character and develop such things as compassion, courage and self-sacrifice. Without evil in the world we would never have such people as Harriet Tubman, Mother Teresa and Gandhi.

God uses the challenges evil brings to draw us to himself and shape us into the kind of people he wants us to be. As Ronald Nash points out, "Most of what we consider significant with regard to human spiritual and moral development arises as a result of interaction with challenge."[9] Through such things as danger, disappointment and loss we have the opportunity to choose to become better or worse people.

When I first began to understand this, I accepted it only grudgingly. *If I have to undergo pain to produce character, so be it,* I thought, but I secretly suspected God could have found a better way. But then I began to wonder if perhaps our participation with God in producing godliness in ourselves actually increases the glory of attainment—the glory for God and our potential for sharing in this glory.

> **It's odd to express appreciation to a wheelchair, but I do. Almost thirty years of quadriplegia, and almost as many studying God's Word, have deepened my gratitude to God for these bolts and bars.**
> **JONI EARECKSON TADA (writer, artist and paralysis victim)[10]**

To help explain this, Nash uses the analogy of someone who wants to climb to the top of Mt. Rainier. But as the person begins arduous training, he decides it is too difficult and instead rents a helicopter to take him to the top. Would reaching the summit without any real effort be even a fraction as meaningful as climbing it would have been?[11] Now consider how this might translate to the spiritual process of soul making. Perhaps if soul making could be accomplished without struggle, it would be far less valuable in the end.

 What difficult situations can you think of that have helped you to grow as a person or draw closer to God?

What is your response to the idea that the effort we are required to invest in our own growth could increase the value in the end?

A Long Road Home

Although the prevalence of evil in the world has been one of the issues I have struggled with most, wrestling with this question has also stretched my understanding of God and myself. The question has led me on a long and winding path, with many switchbacks and confusing loops, but somewhere in the journey my perspective has begun to change. I have gone from suspecting that evil is an indication of the absence of God to realizing that the Christian answer possesses an uncanny ability to fit the pieces of the puzzle of evil together in the only way I can find that begins to make sense.

The Christian answer explains why we sometimes come into contact with a depth of evil that evades all *natural* explanation—gruesome murders, shocking child molestations and bizarre accounts of apparent demon possession. It explains the strange fact that we simultaneously abhor evil and contribute to it—at the minimum through the occasional cruel word or selfish action. It explains why evil persists despite all advancements in society and efforts to eradicate it. It explains and *legitimizes* the fact that even though most of us no longer have any idealistic dreams of ridding the world of all evil, we still feel compelled to eliminate as much evil as possible. And it explains the peculiar reality that true fulfillment seems to come only from self-sacrifice, and yet we find self-sacrifice one of the hardest things to do.

> It is precisely because the Christian faith solves the problem of evil with amazing adequacy that I have become so convinced a Christian. It solves evil in thought; it solves evil in life.
>
> NELS F. S. FERRÉ[12]

I have gone from secretly resenting God for allowing this fallen world and all the pain it entails to harboring a reluctant but increasing appreciation for the grandness and ingenuity of his plan to redeem the world from evil—*allowing us to be part of the process*. I used to struggle with how the Fall fit into God's plan. I viewed Adam and Eve's world as God's original plan for us and the world we live in now as a less-than-optimal plan B. But how could an omniscient God have a plan B? Finally, it struck me that perhaps this *is* plan A. God knew what we would do, he knew what his response would be, and he knew that somehow what is to come would be worth it all. This way raises the stakes, intensifies the conflict, but also exponentially compounds the reward.

My faith still quivers when I come in contact with suffering. I have encountered little true hardship in my life, but what little I have seen reveals how faint-hearted I am. And when I am in the middle of it all, sometimes I find it hard to accept these answers—but perhaps grappling with this at these times is also part of the process of being shaped into who God wants me to be.

Do you agree that Christianity begins fitting pieces of the puzzle of evil together in a way that makes sense? Why or why not? Can you think of some evils in the world that point to the existence of the supernatural? Explain.

Do you think it is impossible for an omniscient God to have a plan B? Explain your thoughts on this subject.

 Do you believe that the existence of evil in the world disproves Christianity? Why or why not?

Digging Deeper

The Problem of Pain *by C. S. Lewis (New York: Macmillan, 1962). This is a mind-and faith-stretching book I highly recommend for those struggling with the question of evil in the world.*

Evil and the Christian God *by Michael Peterson (Grand Rapids, Mich.: Baker, 1982). Peterson comprehensively explores the philosophical arguments for and against Christianity involved in the issue of evil.*

Where Is God When It Hurts? *by Philip Yancey, rev. ed. (Grand Rapids, Mich.; Zondervan, 1990). This revised version of Yancey's classic book explores the often heart-rending questions raised by the existence of pain and offers sensitive advice on how to cope with our own pain and the pain of others.*

Reflections on Religions

But What About Other Religions?

The question naturally arises as to whether or not Christianity is unique among world religions. Or is it only a variation on a basic theme running through all religions?

PAUL LITTLE, *Know Why You Believe*

T he immense hall was dimly lit and sparsely furnished. Arabic inscriptions, elaborate carvings and bright mosaics graced the walls, and the entire floor was covered by an array of patterned rugs fit together like a gigantic jigsaw puzzle. There were no chairs or benches. Most of the people present were dressed in flowing robes and kneeling prostrate on the floor. As I studied the faces of the worshipers there at the Aqsa Mosque in Jerusalem, I couldn't escape the notion that although their religion was quite different from mine, these Muslims were at least as dedicated and sincere as most Christians I know.

Even since I returned to Christianity wholeheartedly, encounters with people of other faiths have raised unsettling questions. It is one thing to believe in the truth of Christianity in my own small world dominated by church activities and Christian friends, but quite another when confronted with people of other faiths who seem just as convinced and sincere in their beliefs. At these times I often ask the same questions I hear many others asking today. Do I really have more reason to believe in the truth of Christianity than in the truth of other religions? Or am I convinced of the truth of Christianity only because it is the belief system most familiar to me? Isn't it arrogant to believe Christianity is the only true religion? And couldn't all religions be different expressions of divine truth?

 What are some encounters you have had with people of other religions, and how have these affected your faith?

Different Expressions of Divine Truth?

The view that all religions are different expressions of divine truth is by far the most popular and politically correct in Western cultures right now. This belief has become so prevalent that many consider it one of the few self-evident facts and see anyone who doesn't agree with this pluralistic outlook as arrogant and narrow-minded. They are willing to tolerate anything except such intolerance. So when I was sorting through questions about other religions, this concept of pluralism was the first possibility I considered.

> In an age of toleration and pluralism, the most popular argument against the Christian religion seems to be simply that it is only one of many religions.
> PETER KREEFT AND RONALD K. TACELLI[1]

I must confess that sometimes I wish pluralism could be true. It is an appealing belief system because it relieves us of the necessity of wrestling with hard questions of truth and of having to concern ourselves with the spiritual fate of others. Many religions share certain moral principles, so it would be easy to equate religion with moral codes and dismiss all of the radical theological differences. But I found I could not believe in pluralism for a number of reasons.

☐ Religion has to do with much more than codes of behavior. Integral to all world religions are concepts of the nature of God, the purpose of humanity, the status of a person after death and the source of ultimate truth. Even the most informal survey of world religions quickly reveals that the essential doctrines of the various religions drastically contradict each other.

☐ Some try to argue that all these theological issues are inconsequential and that true religion involves getting beyond all these differences and attaining some sort of higher truth. But when we look at it, isn't this view simply suggesting another set of religious beliefs and claiming that this belief system is "higher"—in other words, "truer"—than traditional religions with all their theological diversity?

☐ Upon examination pluralism actually contradicts itself. As Brian McLaren explains in *Finding Faith*, each religion claims (either overtly or inadvertently) that it is not just *an* option but *the* option, or at least the *best* option. "If all religions are equally true, as pluralism claims, then each religion is false when it claims that some or all other religions are not true . . . which proves that pluralism (which claims that all religions are equally true) is false when it claims that all religions are true. Does that make sense? It shouldn't!"[2]

☐ Also, if we are going to hold that all beliefs are of equal value, we cannot fudge later by excluding certain beliefs we happen not to like. And I have never yet met a person who didn't see it necessary to condemn some belief systems. Are we really willing to say that the belief system of a tribal chief performing human sacrifice, a white supremacist advocating mass genocide or a Satanist promoting anarchy and lawlessness is of equal value to all other beliefs?

> We live in an age in which tolerance is a key word. Tolerance, however, must be clearly understood. (Truth, by its very nature, is intolerant of error.) If two plus two is four, the total cannot at the same time be twenty-three. . . . One must be tolerant of other points of view and respect their right to be held and heard. He cannot, however, be forced in the name of tolerance to agree that all points of view, including those that are mutually contradictory, are equally valid.
>
> PAUL LITTLE[3]

What are some of the differences among the world religions you are familiar with?

Do you agree that if religions contradict each other they can't all be equally true? Why or why not?

What is your view of pluralism?

Isn't It Arrogant to View Christianity as the Only True Faith?

Belief that Christianity is the only true faith *can be* arrogant if it is motivated by pride and the desire for supremacy. But it is not when encased in humility and motivated solely by the desire to know and live truth. The Bible specifically teaches that Jesus is "the way, the truth and the life" and that no one can come to God except through him (Jn 14:6).

This is not a concept that Christians have gotten together and voted on with the desire to exclude others. It is a basic doctrine that those who believe in the reliability of the Bible cannot ignore. Of course it should never be viewed as an excuse not to demonstrate compassion, meekness and understanding in interactions with people of other faiths. For these also are basic elements of Christianity.

 Do you agree that believing Christianity is the only true religion isn't necessarily arrogant? Why or why not?

What would be the major differences between the words and actions of Christians who are arrogant in this belief and the words and actions of those who are not?

The Options

But realizing that all religions cannot be equally true just led me back to the other questions. My spiritual search had led me to exciting discoveries about Christianity and mind-expanding insights into myself and the world around me. But don't *all people* think their own religion is true? How could I know that Christianity is really any different? How could a person ever learn enough about *all* the other world religions to even make an intelligent comparison?

> Worldviews ... are not infinite in number. In a pluralistic society they seem to exist in profusion, but the basic issues and options are actually rather small.
> JAMES W. SIRE[4]

The thought of trying to investigate the truth claims of all world religions is intimidating, to say the least. However, I was surprised to find that when I began exploring world religions, there were many fewer options than I had imagined. This is not to say that much diversity of belief doesn't exist *even within each religious tradition*. But despite the important differences each religion possesses, I found it is possible to categorize world religions into a handful of basic options regarding their fundamental approaches to God.

 Have you attempted to investigate other religions? If so, in what ways, and what has been the result?

Assessing PEARLs
Prophecy
Can these religions point to well-attested examples of fulfilled prophecy equivalent to those of the Bible?
Experience
Can we see in history and throughout the world today that these religions powerfully change people's lives for the better?
Archaeology
Does archaeology support the historical claims of these religions?
Resurrection
Can these religions point to well-documented confirming miracles in the same way Christianity can point to the resurrection?
Logic
Do these religions give the most consistent, comprehensive and satisfying explanation of humanity and the world?

Polytheism

Polytheists believe in the existence of numerous finite gods. Some polytheists believe these gods arose from nature, while others maintain they were humans who turned into gods. Although the names and characteristics of gods differ among various polytheistic systems, adherents generally view their gods as beings possessing superhuman power but not necessarily superior morality or wisdom. Polytheistic gods are often portrayed as very humanlike in their actions and motives, often fighting among themselves, holding grudges, exacting revenge and deceiving both gods and humans.

> God himself once was as we are now, and is an exalted man, and sits enthroned in yonder heavens! ... And you have got to learn how to be gods yourselves ... the same as all gods have done before you.
>
> JOSEPH SMITH (founder of Mormonism)[5]

There are many examples of polytheistic religions from ancient times—for example, the mythologies of Greece, Rome and Norway. A renewed interest in polytheism has recently arisen in the Western world through what is sometimes called "the new paganism." The beliefs of the Mormon Church are also polytheistic in that Mormonism teaches that many gods exist and that the God Mormons worship was previously a man.

Comments on Polytheism

☐ Most polytheistic systems do not contain any explanation for the beginning of the universe. Their teaching that the gods either were birthed from nature or were once humans leaves unanswered the question of who created nature and the first humans.

☐ Polytheism usually is dualistic in its approach to morality, which leaves no basis for belief in a true "right" and "wrong." Dualism teaches that two groups of independent gods exist, one preferring cruelty and hatred and the other preferring love and mercy. But since neither group created the other or has any claim to supremacy, what is the basis for calling the one group "good" and the other "evil"?

☐ I haven't found any polytheistic religion that can compare with Christianity in the areas of archaeology, fulfilled prophecy, confirming miracles or transformation of lives.

A Face of Polytheism

Ruthann is a social work student at an American university who dabbles in the new paganism. Her religious practices involve magic, nighttime festivals and the worship of numerous gods who possess different personalities and strengths. She explains that the creed of her Wiccan group is "As long as you harm no one, do what you will."

 Do you agree with these comments about polytheism? If not, which ones do you disagree with and why?

If you were to believe in polytheism, what reasons would you have? How do these compare with the reasons for belief in Christianity?

Pantheism

Pantheists believe that God is everything that exists and everything that exists is God. The universe and God are considered to be one and the same thing. God is the absolute reality that unites all things. This reality is impersonal, eternal, unchanging and infinite. Because of this, pantheists believe that God is in all humanity, and individuals can receive power and insight by realizing their divinity and connecting with the divine power everywhere present.

Pantheists maintain that if God is all, then the concept of evil must be an illusion. They believe that on the highest level of understanding, ultimate truth is found in contradiction. The Absolute One is beyond good and evil and at the same time contains them both. Although pantheists often emphasize good actions and self-sacrifice, they believe ultimately that once a person moves beyond the lower levels of spiritual attainment, that person no longer needs to be concerned with moral law. For the pantheist, the highest realization is that there is neither good nor evil.

> So he who understands [wisdom]—by no deed whatsoever of his is his world injured, not by stealing, not by killing an embryo, not by the murder of his mother, not by the murder of his father.
>
> KAUSITAKI UPANISHAD 3.1 (Hindu scripture)[6]

Pantheism generally sees "the Absolute One" as drastically different from anything we know, so we cannot use reason in religious matters. Pantheists practice meditation techniques in an attempt to empty the mind of all thought, contemplating reasonless questions such as "What is the sound of one hand clapping?" or mystical syllables such as "om." These are believed to open the mind to the understanding that everything, even in all its contradictions, is God.

Pantheism is most prevalent in Eastern religions. Many forms of Hinduism, Taoism and Buddhism are pantheistic. And pantheism is becoming much more common in the Western world through the spread of Eastern religions, as well as through the teachings of Christian Science, Unity, Scientology and New Age philosophy. The Star Wars movies are good examples of popular pantheistic thought.

Comments on Pantheism

☐ Even though a basic doctrine of pantheism is that reason can tell us nothing about God, pantheism does selectively apply reason in its teachings. A belief system truly consistent with this premise would just be a conglomeration of unrelated statements with no life application possible. Humans cannot escape the use of reason. It is reason that tells pantheists that God is above reason, and it is reason that allows pantheists to apply this teaching in their lives.

☐ If we are to wholeheartedly accept the pantheistic view, we must wholeheartedly accept the concept that there is no real distinction between good and evil. We must be willing to say it is ultimately just as "good" for me to pour scalding water on someone as it is for me to give my life for him or her. But this belief runs so contrary to our concept of reality that most of us cannot live consistently with it. Even pantheistic literature is filled with moral appeals, despite the fact that this belief system does not ultimately allow for true right and wrong.

☐ Even though many pantheists believe the material world is an illusion, even the most enlightened person cannot disregard matter altogether. For example, even the most enlightened person must eat to live.

☐ Because of pantheism's emphasis on the irrational, it does not easily lend itself to objective support such as prophecy, archaeology and confirming miracles.

Do you agree with these comments about pantheism? If not, which ones do you disagree with and why?

If you were to believe in pantheism, what reasons would you have? How do these compare with reasons for belief in Christianity?

Deism

Deists believe that God created the universe and established the natural laws but then withdrew to allow the universe to develop on its own. Most deists believe that God is personal, all-good, all-loving and all-powerful but that he never interferes with the natural order or intervenes in the lives of people. This view was particularly popular Europe and North American in the eighteenth century, during what is referred to as the Age of Enlightenment. Many founders of the United States embraced this view, including Thomas

Paine, Benjamin Franklin and Thomas Jefferson.

The deist believes that the world is the only revelation we have to tell us of God. Evil is considered the byproduct of blind natural laws and the actions of human beings. Deists generally maintain that God has placed a moral law in human hearts to direct our actions, but since they do not hold to any revelation beyond nature, deists often disagree widely about what this moral code forbids or endorses.

Comments on Deism

☐ Deists give no sufficient reason for accepting the biggest miracle of all—the miracle of creation—but rejecting the possibility of smaller miracles.

☐ Deism raises the monumental question of how an all-powerful, all-loving, all-knowing God would abandon his creation to the kind of depravity and cruelty that exist in the world today.

☐ Since deists reject the possibility of specific divine revelation or supernatural acts, they do not possess any positive evidence for their view such as fulfilled prophecy, confirming miracles or substantiating archeological finds.

☐ Deism has shown itself to be an unstable worldview. Despite the widespread acceptance of this view a few hundred years ago, not many hold to it today.

> A being who could bring the universe into existence from nothing could certainly perform lesser miracles if he chose to do so. A God who created water could part it or make it possible for a person to walk on it. . . . It seems self-defeating to admit a great miracle like creation and then to deny the possibility of lesser miracles.
> NORMAN L. GEISLER[7]

Deism seems to have been a middle step taken by those desiring to relieve humanity of the constraints of religion but not quite willing to give up the comfort of belief in God.

Do you agree with these comments about deism? If not, which ones do you disagree with and why?

If you were to believe in deism, what reasons would you have? How do these compare with the reasons for belief in Christianity?

Monotheism

Monotheism is, of course, the category to which Christianity belongs. Monotheism asserts that there is one personal, transcendent God who has always existed outside of time and space, has created both the universe and humanity and is still intimately involved with both. Only two major monotheistic world religions exist besides Christianity: Judaism and Islam.

Judaism. Most of us are familiar with Judaism because it is the foundation for Christianity. The Jewish Scriptures are revered by Christians and are even included in the Christian Bible. The truth of Christianity partly rests on whether Judaism as taught in the Jewish Scriptures is true. However, Christianity goes a step further in teaching that Jesus was the fulfillment of Judaism.

Judaism is intrinsically linked with the Jewish ethnic group. Adherents to Judaism usually believe that the Jewish people possess a special relationship with God and that acceptance by God is based on being or becoming part of the Jewish community as well as living a righteous life. Although modern Judaism has much diversity and usually emphasizes a way of life rather than specific doctrinal beliefs, the key issue in deciding between Judaism and Christianity is whether you believe that Jesus is the promised Jewish Messiah.

If you were to reject Christianity, would you accept Judaism? Why or why not?

Islam. Islam is second only to Christianity in the number of followers it has in the world today. It was founded by an Arab man named Muhammad about six hundred years after the time of Christ. Those who follow the Islamic faith are called Muslims, which means "ones who submit."

Islam shares some things in common with Judaism and Christianity. Muslims believe in the existence of one transcendent God. They also believe that both the Jewish and Christian Scriptures represent divine revelations. But they believe that these revelations have been corrupted and that now only the Qur'an (Koran), the Islamic holy book, contains the unaltered and final revelation. Muslims believe in the Jewish prophets and patriarchs but emphasize Abraham's son Ishmael rather than Isaac. They believe Jesus was a miracle worker and a prophet but reject his divinity, his death on the cross and his resurrection.

Islam emphasizes the exaltation, supremacy and holiness of God above all else. The relationship between God and human beings is viewed as a relationship between master and slave more than parent and child. The Qur'an teaches that God doesn't love the wayward child or those who do wrong and that the duty of the Muslim is to obey God, not necessarily to know him.

Central to traditional Islam is the concept of strict predestination, meaning that all that happens, both good and bad, is directly willed by God, including all the actions of individual people. Islam teaches God is

> Had it been Our will, We could have given every soul its guidance. But My word shall be fulfilled: "I will surely fill Hell with jinn [angels] and humans all."
> SURA 32:13[8]

Absolute Will—that we can describe his actions but not his essence. He has no characteristics that compel him to act in any specific way. Although considered most merciful and loving, he can be either loving or not as he chooses, and both are considered right.

Muslims believe individuals can earn the right to go to paradise by doing good deeds. However, only God can judge when a person has done enough good deeds, so salvation is never certain unless a person is killed in a holy war while defending or spreading Islam.

Comments on Islam

□ The Qur'an itself refers to the Jewish and Christian Scriptures as authentic (Suras 2:136; 5:45-48) and exhorts Jews and Christians to "observe the Torah and the Gospel and that which has been revealed to you from your Lord" (Sura 5:68). It also states that no one can change the words of God (Sura 6:115). This contradicts the Muslim belief that these scriptures have now been corrupted. And even the passages Muslims point to in the Qur'an to teach such corruption seem to actually speak of the misuse of these texts and attempts to add to them rather than their widespread alteration (Suras 2:75; 2:78-79).

□ No manuscript evidence exists that the Jewish and Christian Scriptures have been altered as the Muslims believe. In fact, abundant evidence exists to the contrary, especially in regard to the New Testament documents (see chapter six). If these Scriptures are still authentic and accurate and yet contradict teachings found in the Qur'an, this presents difficulties for the authenticity of the Qur'an.

☐ Islam also teaches that God created humanity pure in nature and rejects the idea that this nature has been altered by Adam's sin. Islam thus lacks an explanation for the inclination toward selfishness and corruption we see in others and ourselves.

☐ As was discussed in chapter seven, much evidence exists supporting the fact that Jesus claimed to be the Son of God and was raised from the dead. If this is correct, it undermines Islam.

A Face of Islam

Erik had a good friend in college who was a Jordanian Muslim. Abdul was fiercely proud of his family and his Islamic heritage and believed without question that Islam was the most logical religion. It was impossible not to admire Abdul in his strict adherence to Muslim regulations despite being thousands of miles from his home and surrounded by all the temptations of American college life. He even refused to use toothpaste during the fast of Ramadan for fear he would swallow it. Abdul was a champion of Muslim law, defending it and explaining that although it may seem harsh, it is necessary.

Do you agree with these comments about Islam? If not, which ones do you disagree with and why?

If you were to believe in Islam, what reasons would you have? How do these compare with the reasons for believing in Christianity?

Criticism or Compassion?

We were sitting on the floor surrounded by the remains of a delicious Indian meal when the conversation suddenly turned to religion. "I don't have problems with other faiths as long as they don't insist they are the only true one," Charmie, our Hindu hostess, commented. "Christianity doesn't insist it is the only true religion—does it?"

I shifted awkwardly. "Actually," another Christian friend said, "Christianity does teach that Jesus is the only way to get to heaven, and so other religions that disagree with this can't be equally true."

Charmie looked incredulous and began asking questions, launching us into an in-depth discussion of the differences between Hinduism and Christianity. As we left that evening, I hoped the discussion hadn't offended our hostess.

It was several weeks before I saw Charmie again. This time we were at a birthday party for a common friend, and she came running over to greet me before I was even out of the car. Her face was aglow and she gave me a big, unexpected hug. "There is something I have to tell you," she said. "I am a Christian too! I have accepted Christ, and now we are sisters!" The joy in her eyes was unmistakable.

My purpose in this chapter is not to criticize other people's religions. Yet if Christianity is true, the most compassionate thing we can do for others is help them discover this and point them to Christ—just as if I am wrong about Christianity, the best thing someone can do is point out my error so I can find truth elsewhere.

I have been surprised at Christianity's uniqueness. In particular it is the only religion in which "salvation" is not in the least based on a person's good actions but is based solely on the *kindness* of God. And in the areas in which I did find Christianity similar to other religions, it is similar in ways that would be expected if Christianity were true—for instance, in the repeated motif of the need for a sacrifice for wrongdoing and in the unanimous acknowledgment of the moral imperfections of humanity even in religions that consider humanity in some way divine.

> Comparative religion is very comparative indeed. That is, it is so much a matter of degree and distance and difference that it is only comparatively successful when it tries to compare. When we come to look at it closely we find it comparing things that are really quite incomparable. ... In truth the Church is too unique to prove herself unique. For most popular and easy proof is by parallel; and here there is no parallel.
>
> G. K. CHESTERTON[9]

Of course it is impossible to cover all the aspects of the religions of the world in a chapter of this length, and each person must make his or her own decision. But I have discovered that looking into the claims of other faiths has actually *strengthened* my faith in the truth of Christianity.

Can you think of any religions that do not fit in one of the four categories listed in this chapter? If so, explain.

If you were to reject Christianity, what religion do you think you would choose and why?

How does the evidence for this religion compare with that for Christianity?

Do you believe it is possible that all religions are just different expressions of divine truth? Why or why not?
Do you believe Christianity possesses unique evidence to support its claim of truth? Why or why not?

Digging Deeper

Religions of the World: The Illustrated Guide to Origins, Beliefs, Traditions and Festivals *by Elizabeth Breuilly, Joanne O'Brien and Martin Palmer (New York: Facts on File, 1997). A well-illustrated, straightforward overview of the beliefs and practices of world religions.*

Handbook of Today's Religions *by Josh McDowell and Don Stewart (San Bernadino, Calif.: Here's Life, 1989). This is a good resource if you are looking for a basic comparison of world religions from a Christian perspective.*

Eerdmans Handbook to World Religions edited by *Pat Alexander (Grand Rapids, Mich.: Eerdmans, 1994). This resource presents a more in-depth summary of world religions, including ancient pagan religions, from a light-handed Christian perspective.*

A Choice of the Heart

So this is what the Sovereign LORD says:
"See, I lay a stone in Zion,
a tested stone,
a precious cornerstone for a sure foundation;
the one who trusts will never be dismayed."

ISAIAH 28:16

I was struggling with doubt again. At times it seemed I had come so far from that night in the university chapel, and then at other times I seemed to be right back where I'd started. I had just come home from a retreat, and the words of the speaker were still buzzing in my head. In contrast to my turmoil, the speaker had seemed so at peace. In contrast to my discontentment, she had seemed so satisfied. In contrast to my weariness, she had seemed to be bubbling over with a quiet but inexhaustible joy.

It was February and still chilly, but I went outside and sat alone on the steps of our deck. I had been challenged by the speaker's faith and by her simple trust in God. Why couldn't I have that? In previous years I had looked into evidences for Christianity and had been convinced of their sufficiency, but sometimes doubt still sneaked up and waylaid me before I even saw it coming. What was I missing?

Was it really possible to live in close communion with God? Was it really possible to experience his power in my life? Was it possible to believe that he loves me more than I could ever love anyone? Was it possible that I could really possess the peace that transcends all understanding?

Then I noticed a disturbing trend in my thoughts. At least in some way for as long as I could remember, I had always been questioning. I had made a decision to follow God and trusted him with my soul, but on a daily basis I did not live in that trust. It suddenly struck me how many times the Bible commands us to believe (Prov 3:5; Mk 5:36; Heb 10:23). I had fallen into the trap of subconsciously thinking that what I believed was not necessarily something I had control over. But now as I considered various Bible passages, I couldn't escape the notion that believing must be something I could *choose* to do.

 What is your response to the idea that believing is something we can choose to do?

The Choice in Faith
God doesn't ask us to produce faith in a vacuum. As was discussed in chapter two, healthy faith is firmly grounded in reality. We need to ask questions and know what the foundation is for belief in Christ. But then we *must* make a choice. If no amount of investigation is enough for us and we are never willing to make a decision based on the answers we find, our investigation is useless. Unfortunately, not to decide to believe is the same as deciding not to believe.

Rationale + Choice = Faith?
While the equation of faith includes the elements of rationale and choice, this is not all it includes. The Bible teaches that there is also a mystifying divine element at work that is beyond the scope of human grasp. Who can understand this incomprehensible soul-talk of God's drawing us, revealing truth and giving capacity

for belief? It is the combination of these elements that can culminate in a life-changing faith—a wholehearted surrender of the inner being.

Faith is a choice. Realizing this has been revolutionary in my life. Faith is a decision—not just of the mind but of the whole being—when we first come to Christ, and our choice does not end there. Choosing to believe is a continual process in the life of faith. When we stop deciding to believe, our Christian growth stalls and our faith stagnates.

This is not to say that once we become Christians all inquiry should stop. Healthy investigation is crucial to a growing faith. As Os Guinness explains in *In Two Minds*, "Different stages of our lives need different levels of comprehension to match our growth and maturity. . . . The challenges to faith will go on and must go on being answered."[1] Yet we shouldn't abandon our faith every time we don't understand something. At this point our inquiry should be performed from inside our faith.

 Do you agree that choosing to believe is a continual process in the life of faith? Why or why not?

How does it work for a person to explore additional questions from within the framework of faith?

The Role of the Will

Key to continuing in the choice of faith is understanding that the life of faith must be lived in the will, not the emotions. Many times I try to live it the other way around without even realizing it. When I am surrounded by Christian friends and feel happy and spiritual, I overflow with faith. But when I encounter something difficult or feel gloomy and unspiritual, my faith suddenly evaporates, and I find myself in a desert of doubt and despair. Many times nothing objective has really changed; I still have the same reasons for believing Christianity is true. Only my *feelings* have changed.

As Guinness writes, "Out-voted, out-gunned, faith is pressed back and hemmed in by the unruly mob of raging emotions which only a while earlier were quiet, orderly citizens of the personality. Reason is cut down, obedience is thrown out, and for a while the rule of the emotions is as sovereign as it is violent."[2]

But it doesn't have to be this way. Our emotions don't have to have the final say. It is our will, not our emotions, that governs us. As Hannah Whitall Smith explains, "It is sometimes thought that the emotions are the governing power in our nature. But I think we all of us know . . . that there is something within us, behind our emotions and behind our wishes, an independent self, that, after all, decides everything and controls everything."[3]

> The common thought is that this life hid with Christ in God is to be lived in the emotions, and consequently all the attention of the soul is directed toward them, and as they are satisfactory or otherwise, the soul rests or is troubled. Now, the truth is, that this life is not to be lived in the emotions at all, but in the will; and therefore, if only the will is kept steadfastly abiding in its center, God's will, the varying states of emotion do not in the least disturb or affect the reality of the life.
> HANNAH WHITALL SMITH[4]

I don't think I have ever experienced this more vividly than when I went rappelling in Alaska with some friends. They carefully demonstrated how to put on the harness and use the ropes. I had seen them go down safely before me. I was confident that I understood the instructions, and I didn't doubt that the rope was strong enough to hold me. But when it actually came time to jump backwards off the side of the cliff, I was so scared I could hardly breathe. It took every ounce of willpower I had to overrule the fear and take that backward jump. *But I did it!*

In a similar way we can choose to rein in our emotions in matters of faith and decide to believe the truth we know. Our will can choose to let our emotions dictate to our faith, or it can choose to let our faith dictate to our emotions. Our emotions may protest, but in the end, when we set our will on a particular path, our emotions follow. And it is the decision of our will that God considers the decision of our selves—regardless of how unruly our emotions may be.

Are Emotions the Enemy?

Saying that we shouldn't always follow our emotions in matters of faith doesn't mean that our emotions are not valuable. Our emotions are God-given and are an intrinsic part of our being. For example, without the emotion of fear I might rappel off the side of a cliff without ever checking my rope.

Also, our emotions will not always be in contrast to our faith. Sometimes it is our very emotions that cry out for God. As the psalmist wrote, "My soul thirsts for God, for the living God" (Ps 42:2).

Have you experienced times when your faith has turned to doubt without any objective reason? If so, describe some of the circumstances surrounding these times.

When has your will had to overrule your emotions to complete a task?

Do you agree that the life of faith should be lived in the will rather than the emotions? Why or why not?

Four Things to Do When Doubt Strikes

1. Prayerfully identify the source of doubt.

2. Remind yourself why you believe and ask yourself if this new question might change or outweigh these reasons. (Your journal can help you with this.)

3. If the answer is no, make a conscious decision to believe, even as you attempt to find answers to the new question.

4. If the answer is yes, ask yourself what you need to do to resolve this question— and then do it.

An Experiment

That day on the deck I was very discouraged. However, insight into the choice involved in faith seemed to offer a glimmer of hope. I wondered if it really could make any difference, but I saw no option but to give it a try. So I rallied just enough determination to decide to make continually choosing to believe and living in the reality of that belief my top priority for at least the next two weeks. I felt strangely as if I were diving blindfolded off a steep cliff, hoping beyond hope that the refreshing pool of God's love was really waiting for me below.

I could never have imagined how my life would change in those weeks. It was as if I had never before tasted the fullness of Christianity. When doubt threatened, I examined the doubt, compared it with the truth I knew, and chose to

> Trust in the dark, trust in the light, trust at night and trust in the morning, and you will find that the faith that may begin perhaps by a mighty effort will end, sooner or later, by becoming the easy and natural habit of the soul. It is a law of the spiritual life that every act of trust makes the next act less difficult, until at length, if these acts are persisted in, trusting becomes, like breathing, the natural unconscious action of the redeemed soul.
>
> HANNAH WHITALL SMITH[5]

For this reason I kneel before the Father.... I pray that out of his glorious riches he may strengthen you with power through his Spirit in your inner being, so that Christ may dwell in your hearts through faith. And I pray that you, being rooted and established in love, may have power, together with all the saints, to grasp how wide and long and high and deep is the love of Christ, and to know this love that surpasses knowledge— that you may be filled to the measure of all the fullness of God.
EPHESIANS 3:14-19

believe God and live in obedience to that belief. I chose to believe God loved me. I chose to believe God had forgiven me. I chose to believe that God was completing his work in me through the power of his Holy Spirit. And I chose to believe that he heard me when I prayed and that his plan was always best.

Before this time I had been frustrated by all the promises about peace and joy in the Bible. But by the end of those two weeks I was able to catch a glimpse of this peace and joy and know for myself that these weren't just idealistic promises but solid realities for those who chose to live in faith.

I would like to be able to say that since that afternoon I have always continued in the practice of choosing faith. I must admit, however, that sometimes I get discouraged and distracted. I am still very much in the process of building the habit of faith in my life. But I *can* say that I have experienced too much of the peace, joy, contentment and power that this choice brings to ever desire to give up the quest.

Where from Here?

You have covered much information in this book. But all the time you have invested in working through it will be wasted if after you finish the last sentence you simply put it down and walk away. Here are some things you can do to continue your journey.

1. Nurture your faith. *Read the Bible and faith-stretching books; spend time in prayer and attempt to live in obedience to your faith; attend a good church and develop friendships with other Christians; challenge yourself in areas that will stretch your faith. As C. S. Lewis writes, "We have to be continually reminded of what we believe. Neither this belief nor any other will automatically remain alive in the mind. It must be fed."*[6]

2. Determine to practice the choice of faith, starting today. *If this seems a big step, try just making the decision to do it for at least two weeks, as I did. At the end of two weeks, you can reassess and decide whether to continue.*

3. Continue seeking answers to your questions. *Go back through your journal*

and take note of the questions you still have. Then think through what you will need to do to answer these questions and determine the bearing they have on your faith.

Do you think sufficient reason exists for belief in Christianity? Why or why not?

Have you chosen or are you ready to choose to trust in the God of Christianity? If so, on what are you basing this decision?

Do you need to investigate anything further before you are ready to decide? If so, what specifically do you need to investigate? What is the next step you need to take?

Digging Deeper

The Christian's Secret of a Happy Life *by Hannah Whitall Smith (Grand Rapids, Mich.: Revell, 1966). Written by a Quaker woman in the 1800s, this powerful little book, still in print over one hundred years later, offers practical instruction on how to find true fulfillment through the choice of faith.*

Beyond Ourselves *by Catherine Marshall (New York: McGraw-Hill, 1961). This spiritual autobiography recounts Marshall's adventure in faith and gives practical instruction, especially in the areas discussed in this chapter, on establishing a more meaningful relationship with God.*

In Two Minds: The Dilemma of Doubt and How to Resolve It *by Os Guinness (Downers Grove, Ill.: InterVarsity Press, 1977). This thorough book explores the relationship between faith and doubt, identifies seven basic kinds of doubt and proposes ways to resolve each of them.*

Notes

Chapter 1: Somewhere Between Belief & Disbelief

[1]Gary R. Habermas, *Dealing with Doubt* (Chicago: Moody Press, 1990), p. 13.

[2]Os Guinness, *In Two Minds: The Dilemma of Doubt and How to Resolve It* (Downers Grove, Ill.: InterVarsity Press, 1976), pp. 108-9.

[3]Allan Bloom, *The Closing of the American Mind* (New York: Simon & Schuster, 1987), p. 381.

[4]Josh McDowell, *More Than a Carpenter* (Wheaton, Ill.: Tyndale House, 1977), p. 39.

[5]C. S. Lewis, "Reflections on the Psalms," in *The Inspirational Writings of C. S. Lewis* (New York: Inspirational, 1994), p. 145.

Chapter 2: Grappling with Doubt

[1]Os Guinness, *In Two Minds: The Dilemma of Doubt and How to Resolve It* (Downers Grove, Ill.: InterVarsity Press, 1976), p. 112.

[2]Clark Pinnock, *A Case for Faith,* quoted in Gary E. Parker, *The Gift of Doubt: From Crisis to Authentic Faith* (San Francisco: Harper & Row, 1990), p. 86.

[3]Paul Little, *Know Why You Believe* (Colorado Springs: Victor/Chariot, 1987), p. 19.

[4]Rufus Jones, *The Radiant Life,* quoted in Parker, *Gift of Doubt,* pp. 71-72.

[5]C. S. Lewis, "Religion: Reality or Substitute," in *Christian Reflections,* ed. Walter Hooper (London: Geoffrey Bles, 1967), p. 41.

[6]Parker, *Gift of Doubt,* p. 30.

[7]Francis Bacon, in *The New Dictionary of Thoughts,* comp. Tryon Edwards and others (n.p.: Standard, 1965), p. 153.

[8]G. Baily, in *New Dictionary of Thoughts,* comp. Edwards and others, p. 154.

Chapter 3: Thoughts on Thinking

[1]Brian D. McLaren, *Finding Faith: A Self-Discovery Guide for Your Spiritual Quest* (Grand Rapids, Mich.: Zondervan, 1999), p. 51.

[2]David Kelley, *The Art of Reasoning* (New York: W. W. Norton, 1988), p. 5.

[3]Ibid., p. 1.

[4]Clark Pinnock, *A Case for Faith,* quoted in Gary E. Parker, *The Gift of Doubt: From Crisis to Authentic Faith* (San Francisco: Harper & Row, 1990), p. 86.

[5]McLaren, *Finding Faith,* p. 58.

[6]Parker, *Gift of Doubt,* pp. 73-74.

[7]Pablo Picasso, quoted in Arianna Stassinopoulos Huffington, *Picasso: Creator and Destroyer* (New York: Simon & Schuster, 1988), p. 438.

[8]Francis A. Schaeffer, *The God Who Is There* (Downers Grove, Ill.: InterVarsity Press, 1968), p. 55.

Chapter 4: The Brushstrokes of God

[1]Mortimer Adler, *Great Books of the Western World*, ed. Robert Maynard Hutchins (Chicago: Encyclopaedia Britannica, 1952), 2:543.

[2]Isaac Newton, *Philosophiae Naturalis Principia Mathematica* (1687), quoted in Paul Davies, *The Mind of God: The Scientific Basis for a Rational World* (New York: Simon & Schuster, 1992), p. 201.

[3]Albert Einstein in Lincoln Barnett, *The Universe and Dr. Einstein,* quoted in Paul Little, *Know Why You Believe* (Colorado Springs: Victor/Chariot, 1987), p. 24.

[4]Charles Darwin, *On the Origin of Species by Means of Natural Selection* (New York: P. F. Collier and Son, 1937), p. 181.

[5]Patrick Glynn, *God: The Evidence—The Reconciliation of Faith and Reason in a Postsecular World* (Rocklin, Calif.: Prima, 1997), p. 19.

[6]Paul Davies, *The Mind of God: The Scientific Basis for a Rational World* (New York: Simon & Schuster, 1992), p. 16.

[7]Glynn, *God*, p. 24.

[8]Richard Morris, *The Fate of the Universe*, quoted in Fred Heeren, *Show Me God: What the Message from Space Is Telling Us About God* (Wheeling, Ill.: Searchlight, 1995), p. 182.

[9]Fred Hoyle, *The Intelligent Universe: A New View of Creation and Evolution* (New York: Holt, Rinehart & Winston, 1984), pp. 11-12.

[10]Paul Davies, *God and the New Physics* (New York: Simon & Schuster, 1983), p. 174.

[11]Heeren, *Show Me God*, pp. 209-19.

[12]John Polkinghorne, *Belief in God in an Age of Science* (New Haven, Conn.: Yale University Press, 1998), p. 10.

[13]Robert T. Rood and James S. Trefil, *Are We Alone? The Possibility of Extraterrestrial Civilizations*, quoted in Heeren, *Show Me God*, p. 220.

[14]William Lane Craig and Quentin Smith, *Theism, Atheism and Big Bang Cosmology* (New York: Oxford University Press, 1993), pp. 4-35.

[15]Davies, *Mind of God*, p. 47.

[16]C. D. Broad, "Kant's Mathematical Antinomies," quoted in William Lane Craig, "Finitude of the Past and God's Existence," in Craig and Smith, *Theism, Atheism and Big Bang Cosmology*, p. 58.

[17]Robert Jastrow, *God and the Astronomers* (New York: W. W. Norton, 1978), pp. 113-14.

[18]George Barna, *The Second Coming of the Church* (Nashville: Word, 1998), p. 67.

[19]C. S. Lewis, *Mere Christianity* (New York: Macmillan, 1952), p. 35.

Chapter 5: Mirrors of Our Maker

[1]Eugène Ionesco, in *The Columbia Dictionary of Quotations,* in *Microsoft Bookshelf Reference Library 1998* (Redmond, Wash.: Microsoft, 1997).

[2]Paul Davies, *The Mind of God: The Scientific Basis for a Rational World* (New York: Simon & Schuster, 1992), p. 20.

[3]John D. Barrow, *Theories of Everything: The Quest for Ultimate Explanation*, quoted in Davies, *Mind of God*, p. 149.

[4]John Polkinghorne, *Belief in God in an Age of Science* (New Haven, Conn.: Yale University Press, 1998), p. 4.

[5]Ibid., pp. 18-19.

[6]C. S. Lewis, *Miracles: How God Intervenes in Nature and Human Affairs* (New York: Macmillan, 1960), p. 18.

[7]John C. Eccles, "The Evolution of Purpose," in *Evidence of Purpose: Scientists Discover the Creator,* ed. John Marks Templeton (New York: Continuum, 1994), pp. 128-29.

[8]Bertrand Russell, "A Free Man's Worship," quoted in John Hick, *Arguments for the Existence of God* (New York: Herder & Herder, 1971), pp. 61-62.

[9]Bertrand Russell, "Human Society in Ethics and Politics," quoted in Hick, *Arguments*, p. 61.

[10]See Lewis, *Mere Christianity*, pp. 18-19.

[11]Augustine, *The Confessions of Saint Augustine* (Springdale, Penn.: Whitaker House, 1996), p. 11.

Chapter 6: Reliable, Relative or Ridiculous

[1]Brian D. McLaren, *Finding Faith: A Self-Discovery Guide for Your Spiritual Quest* (Grand Rapids, Mich.: Zondervan, 1999), p. 232.

[2]See R. T. Beckwith, "The Canon of the Old Testament," in *The Origin of the Bible*, ed. Philip Wesley Comfort (Wheaton, Ill.: Tyndale House, 1992).

[3]Josephus, *Against Apion,* quoted in Gleason L. Archer, *A Survey of Old Testament Introduction* (Chicago: Moody Press, 1994), pp. 79-80.

[4]Milton Fisher, "The Canon of the New Testament," in *The Origin of the Bible,* ed. Philip Wesley Comfort (Wheaton, Ill.: Tyndale House, 1992), p. 73.

[5]R. K. Harrison, "Old Testament and New Testament Apocrypha," in *The Origin of the Bible,* ed. Philip Wesley Comfort (Wheaton, Ill.: Tyndale House, 1992), p. 93.

[6]Josephus, *Against Apion,* quoted in Josh McDowell, *The Best of Josh McDowell: A Ready Defense,* comp. Bill Wilson (Nashville: Thomas Nelson, 1993), p. 36.

[7]See Archer, *Survey of Old Testament Introduction,* pp. 67-73.

[8]Randall Price, *Secrets of the Dead Sea Scrolls* (Eugene, Ore.: Harvest House, 1996), p. 145.

[9]Archer, *Survey of Old Testament Introduction,* p. 29.

[10]Philip Wesley Comfort, "Texts and Manuscripts of the New Testament," in *The Origin of the Bible,* ed. Philip Wesley Comfort (Wheaton, Ill.: Tyndale House, 1992), p. 182.

[11]See Randel McCraw Helms, *Who Wrote the Gospels?* (Altadena, Calif.: Millennium, 1997).

Chapter 7: Grave Issues

[1]John Romer, *Testament: The Bible and History* (New York: Henry Holt, 1988), p. 166.

[2]Michael Collins and Matthew A. Price, *The Story of Christianity: A Celebration of 2,000 Years of Faith* (New York: DK, 1999), p. 7.

[3]Suetonius, *Lives of the Caesars,* quoted in Josh McDowell, *The Best of Josh McDowell: A Ready Defense,* comp. Bill Wilson (Nashville: Thomas Nelson, 1993), p. 200.

[4]Cornelius Tacitus, *Annals,* quoted in Josh McDowell, *The Best of Josh McDowell: A Ready*

Defense, comp. Bill Wilson (Nashville: Thomas Nelson, 1993), p. 198.

[5]Eusebius, *Epistles,* quoted in J. Stevenson, *A New Eusebius* (London: SPCK, 1987), p. 19.

[6]"The New Testament Dating Game," *Time,* March 21, 1977, p. 95.

[7]Paul L. Maier, *First Easter,* quoted in Josh McDowell, *The Resurrection Factor* (Nashville: Thomas Nelson, 1981), p. 27.

[8]Romer, *Testament,* p. 171.

[9]Clark H. Pinnock, *Biblical Revelation* (Chicago: Moody Press, 1971), p. 48.

[10]Craig Blomberg, *The Historical Reliability of the Gospels* (Downers Grove, Ill.: InterVarsity Press, 1987), p. 66.

[11]Romer, *Testament,* p. 178.

Chapter 8: Stones & Scrolls

[1]Edwin M. Yamauchi, "Stones, Scripts and Scholars," quoted in Josh McDowell, *The New Evidence That Demands a Verdict* (Nashville: Thomas Nelson, 1999), p. 92.

[2]Norm Geisler and Ron Brooks, *When Skeptics Ask: A Handbook of Christian Evidences* (Grand Rapids, Mich.: Baker, 1996), pp. 179-80.

[3]Randall Price, *The Stones Cry Out* (Eugene, Ore.: Harvest House, 1997), p. 332.

[4]Peter Kreeft and Ronald K. Tacelli, *Handbook of Christian Apologetics* (Downers Grove, Ill.: InterVarsity Press, 1994), p. 217.

[5]W. F. Albright, *The Archaeology of Palestine,* quoted in McDowell, *New Evidence,* p. 61.

[6]Price, *Stones Cry Out,* p. 83.

[7]See Bryant G. Wood, " 'Did the Israelites Conquer Jericho?' A New Look at the Archaeological Evidence," *Biblical Archaeological Review* 16, no. 2 (March/April 1990): 44-59.

[8]Ibid., p. 152.

[9]A. N. Sherwin-White, *Roman Society and Roman Law in the New Testament,* quoted in Geisler and Brooks, *When Skeptics Ask,* p. 202.

[10]Josh McDowell, *The Best of Josh McDowell: A Ready Defense,* comp. Bill Wilson (Nashville: Thomas Nelson, 1993), pp. 199-200.

[11]Millar Burrows, "How Archaeology Helps the Student of the Bible," quoted in McDowell, *New Evidence,* p. 100.

[12]Norman Geisler, *Baker Encyclopedia of Christian Apologetics* (Grand Rapids, Mich.: Baker, 1999), p. 52.

Chapter 9: What Profit in Prophets

[1]According to J. Barton Payne, *Encyclopedia of Biblical Prophecy* (Grand Rapids, Mich.: Baker, 1973), p. 681.

[2]Norman L. Geisler, *Baker Encyclopedia of Christian Apologetics* (Grand Rapids, Mich.: Baker, 1999), p. 613.

[3]Philip Myers, *General Histories for College and High Schools,* quoted in Josh McDowell, *The Best of Josh McDowell: A Ready Defense,* comp. Bill Wilson (Nashville: Thomas Nelson, 1993), p. 61.

[4]Randall Price, *Secrets of the Dead Sea Scrolls* (Eugene, Ore.: Harvest House, 1996), p. 162.

[5]Ibid.

[6]Gleason L. Archer, *A Survey of Old Testament Introduction* (Chicago: Moody Press, 1994), pp. 430-36.

[7]Ibid., p. 445.

[8]Michel de Nostradamus, *Centuries,* quoted in James Randi, *The Mask of Nostradamus* (New York: Charles Scribner's Sons, 1990), p. 244.

[9]Geisler, *Baker Encyclopedia*, p. 615.

[10]Henry M. Morris with Henry M. Morris III, *Many Infallible Proofs: Evidences for the Christian Faith* (Green Forest, Ark.: Master Books, 1996), p. 190.

Chapter 10: Testing the Track Record

[1]William Wilberforce, quoted in Luis Palau, *God Is Relevant: Finding Strength and Peace in Today's World* (New York: Doubleday, 1997), p. 176.

[2]D. James Kennedy and Jerry Newcombe, *What If Jesus Had Never Been Born?* (Nashville: Thomas Nelson, 1994), p. 206.

[3]C. S. Lewis, *Mere Christianity* (New York: Macmillan, 1952), pp. 175-83.

[4]Paul Johnson, "A Historian Looks at Jesus," quoted in Kennedy and Newcombe, *What If Jesus*, p. 223.

[5]Kennedy and Newcombe, *What If Jesus*, p. 205.

[6]Ibid., pp. 10-14.

[7]Ibid., pp. 40-56.

[8]Tim LaHaye, *Jesus—Who Is He?* (Sisters, Ore.: Multnomah Press, 1996), p. 17.

[9]Kennedy and Newcombe, *What If Jesus*, pp. 18-22.

[10]Craig S. Keener, *Paul, Women and Wives* (Peabody, Mass.: Hendrickson, 1992), p. 6.

[11]H. F. R. Catherwood, *The Christian in Industrial Society,* quoted in Daniel H. Osmond, "A Physiologist Looks at Purpose and Meaning in Life," in *Evidence of Purpose,* ed. John Marks Templeton (New York: Continuum, 1994), p. 137.

[12] Some names have been changed in order to protect the privacy of the individuals.

[13]William Dyrness, *Christian Apologetics in a World Community* (Downers Grove, Ill.: InterVarsity Press, 1983), pp. 65-66.

Chapter 11: God Beyond the Telescope

[1]Francis Bacon, quoted in D. James Kennedy and Jerry Newcombe, *What If Jesus Had Never Been Born?* (Nashville: Thomas Nelson, 1994), p. 97.

[2]D. James Kennedy and Jerry Newcombe, *What If the Bible Had Never Been Written?* (Nashville: Thomas Nelson, 1998), p. 106.

[3]Ibid., p. 104.

[4]Ibid., p. 107.

[5]Isaac Newton, quoted in Kennedy and Newcombe, *What If Jesus,* p. 100.

[6]Ibid., p. 99.

[7]National Academy of Sciences Committee on Science and Creationism, *Science and Creationism: A View from the National Academy of Sciences* (Washington, D.C.: National Academy Press, 1984), p. 6.

[8]George Gaylord Simpson, quoted in Phillip E. Johnson, *Darwin on Trial,* 2nd ed. (Downers

Grove, Ill.: InterVarsity Press, 1993), p. 116.

[9]Francis Bacon, quoted in Charles Colson and Nancy Pearcey, *How Now Shall We Live?* (Wheaton, Ill.: Tyndale House, 1999), p. 69.

[10]Michael Denton, *Evolution: A Theory in Crisis* (Bethesda, Md.: Adler & Adler, 1986), p. 86.

[11]Carl Sagan, quoted in Paul Little, *Know Why You Believe* (Colorado Springs: Victor/Chariot, 1987), p. 95.

[12]C. S. Lewis, *Miracles: How God Intervenes in Nature and Human Affairs* (New York: Macmillan, 1960), p. 68.

[13]Peter Kreeft and Ronald K. Tacelli, *Handbook of Christian Apologetics* (Downers Grove, Ill.: InterVarsity Press, 1994), p. 213.

[14]Lewis, *Miracles,* p. 48.

[15]C. Stephen Evans, *The Quest for Faith,* quoted in Ronald Nash, *Faith and Reason: Searching for a Rational Faith* (Grand Rapids, Mich.: Zondervan, 1988), p. 206.

[16]Lewis, *Miracles,* p. 167.

[17]Blaise Pascal, quoted in Kennedy and Newcombe, *What If Jesus Had Never Been Born?* p. 99.

[18]Norman Geisler, *Baker Encyclopedia of Christian Apologetics* (Grand Rapids, Mich.: Baker, 1999), p. 691.

Chapter 12: Contending with a Tragic World

[1]C. S. Lewis, *The Problem of Pain* (New York: Macmillan, 1962), p. 28.

[2]Peter Kreeft and Ronald K. Tacelli, *Handbook of Christian Apologetics* (Downers Grove, Ill.: InterVarsity Press, 1994), p. 126.

[3]Lewis, *Problem of Pain,* pp. 77-79.

[4]Francis A. Schaeffer, *Genesis in Space and Time* (Downers Grove, Ill.: InterVarsity Press, 1972), p. 100.

[5]Lewis, *Problem of Pain,* p. 76.

[6]Kreeft and Tacelli, *Handbook of Christian Apologetics,* p. 135.

[7]Lewis, *Problem of Pain,* p. 71.

[8]Ibid., p. 93.

[9]Ronald Nash, *Faith and Reason: Searching for a Rational Faith* (Grand Rapids, Mich.: Zondervan, 1988), p. 205.

[10]Joni Eareckson Tada, *Heaven: Your Real Home* (Grand Rapids, Mich.: Zondervan, 1995), p. 9.

[11]Nash, *Faith and Reason,* p. 205.

[12]Nels F. S. Ferré, *Evil and the Christian Faith* (New York: Harper & Brothers, 1947), p. ix.

Chapter 13: Reflections on Religions

[1]Peter Kreeft and Ronald K. Tacelli, *Handbook of Christian Apologetics* (Downers Grove, Ill.: InterVarsity Press, 1994), pp. 342-43.

[2]Brian D. McLaren, *Finding Faith: A Self-Discovery Guide for Your Spiritual Quest* (Grand Rapids, Mich.: Zondervan, 1999), pp. 148-49.

[3]Paul E. Little, *Know Why You Believe* (Colorado Springs: Victor/Chariot, 1984), p. 126.

[4]James W. Sire, *The Universe Next Door: A Basic Worldview Catalog,* 3rd ed. (Downers Grove, Ill.: InterVarsity Press, 1997), p. 195.

[5]Joseph Smith Jr., *The History of the Church of Jesus of Latter-day Saints,* quoted in Norman Geisler and Ron Brooks, *When Skeptics Ask: A Handbook on Christian Evidences* (Grand Rapids, Mich.: Baker, 1996), p. 54.

[6]Kausitaki Upanishad, quoted in Jacob Neusner, ed., *Evil and Suffering* (Cleveland, Ohio: Pilgrim, 1998), p. 17.

[7]Norman L. Geisler, *Baker Encyclopedia of Christian Apologetics* (Grand Rapids, Mich.: Baker, 1999), p. 191.

[8]N. J. Dawood, trans., *The Koran, Translated with Notes* (London: Penguin, 1997), p. 292.

[9]G. K. Chesterton, *The Everlasting Man* (Garden City, N.Y.: Doubleday/Image, 1955), pp. 86-87.

Chapter 14: A Choice of the Heart

[1]Os Guinness, *In Two Minds: The Dilemma of Doubt and How to Resolve It* (Downers Grove, Ill.: InterVarsity Press, 1976), p. 109.

[2]Ibid., p. 154.

[3]Hannah Whitall Smith, *The Christian's Secret of a Happy Life* (1870; reprint Old Tappan, N.J.: Revell, 1966), p. 57.

[4]Ibid.

[5]Ibid., p. 55.

[6]C. S. Lewis, *Mere Christianity* (New York: Macmillan, 1952), p. 124.